Soundings

Issue 10

Windrush
Echoes

EDITORS
Stuart Hall
Doreen Massey
Michael Rustin

GUEST EDITORS
Gail Lewis and Lola Young

POETRY EDITOR
Carole Satyamurti

REVIEWS EDITORS
Becky Hall and
Susanna Rustin

ART EDITOR
Tim Davison

EDITORIAL OFFICE
Lawrence & Wishart
99a Wallis Road
London E9 5LN

MARKETING CONSULTANT
Mark Perryman

ADVERTISEMENTS
Write for information to Soundings,
c/o Lawrence & Wishart

SUBSCRIPTIONS
1998/9 subscription rates are (for three issues):
UK: Institutions £70, Individuals £35
Rest of the world: Institutions £80, Individuals £45

ISSN 1362 6620
ISBN 085315 886 X

Text setting Art Services, Norwich
Cover photograph: © David A. Bailey

Printed in Great Britain by
Cambridge University Press, Cambridge

Soundings is published three
times a year, in autumn,
spring and summer by:
Soundings Ltd
c/o Lawrence & Wishart
99a Wallis Road
London E9 5LN

CONTENTS

——————— *Continued on next page* ———————

Continued from previous page

NOTES ON CONTRIBUTORS

Nadje S. Al-Ali was involved in the Egyptian women's movement before researching it for her PhD, and is now a researcher at the Centre of Migration Studies at the University of Sussex. Half-Iraqi, half german she is concerned with cultural stereotypes about Muslims but also about Westerners. She has been a member of WAF since 1994.

Sonia Boyce is an artist living and working in London.

Phillip Cole is a Principal Lecturer in political philosophy at Middlesex University.

Alan Finlayson is a Lecturer in the School of Politics, Queen's University,Belfast. He is the author of a number of articles on theories of politics, ideology and nationalism and is currently writing a book on the concept of community in political thought.

Will Forrest is a writer who has extensive experience, at the receiving end, of the British mental health system.

Femi Franklin lived in North London and worked in the science laboratory of a school. He was extremely interested in all aspects of photography, and had a passion for old cameras. He died in 1994.

Sean Gray is an economist who has worked in politics and government.

Stuart Hall is joint editor of *Soundings*.

Simon Hamilton-Clarke attends Hatch End High School and lives in Harrow with his mother, father, sister and brother.

Jackie Kay is a poet who lives in Manchester. Her first novel *Trumpet* was published this year by Picador.

Michael Laskey lives in Suffolk, where he is co-ordinator of the Aldeburgh Poetry Festival, and co-editor of the poetry magazine, *Smiths Knoll*. He has published two volumes of poetry, of which the most recent is *The Tightrope Wedding*.

Gail Lewis is a Lecturer in Social Policy at the Open University.

Aasiya Lodhi is a writer and a researcher currently working on *East Asia Today*.

Bilkis Malek contributed to *Young Britain: Politics, Pleasures and Predicaments*, Jonathan Rutherford (ed), published by Lawrence & Wishart in 1998; she is currently completing her doctoral thesis.

Richard Moncrieff is completing his PhD at Southampton University; he has returned recently from a research trip to Africa.

Roshi Naidoo is a part-time lecturer in Literature and Cultural Studies at Middlesex University.

Dorothy Nimmo's most recent volume of poetry, *The Children's Game*, was a Poetry Book Society Recommendation for Spring, 1998. She won a Cholmondely Award for Poetry in 1996.

Mike Phillips is a novelist and critic. His most recent novel is *The Dancing Face*, published by Harper Collins. He is co-author with Trevor Phillips of *Windrush: the irresistible rise of multi-racial Britain*.

Anne Phoenix teaches psychology at Birbeck College, University of London.

Mario Pianta is an economist at the National Research Council and at the University of Urbino. He writes for the daily *Il Manifesto* and is active with the association Lunaria.

David Sibley teaches cultural geography at the University of Hull. He is author of *Geographies of Exclusion*, Routledge 1995.

Julia Sudbury is an assistant professor in ethnic studies at Mills College, Oakland, California. She worked as co-ordinator for the Osaba Women's Centre in Coventry; the experience inspired her book *Other Kinds of Dreams: Black Women's Organisations and the Politics of Transformation* (Routledge, 1998).

Stephen Wade lectures in English Studies at the University of Huddersfield. He has published two volumes of poetry.

Susan Wicks is the author of three collections of poetry, the most recent of which, *The Clever Daughter*, was a Poetry Book Society Choice, and was short-listed for both the TS Eliot and Forward prizes. She has also published a memoir, *Driving my Father*, and her second novel, *Little Thing*, was published by Faber in May 1998.

Val Wilmer is a journalist and a photographer and the author of several books on black music. She is working on a history of Black British musicians and has written an entry on the subject for the forthcoming *Encyclopaedia Africana*.

Lola Young is Professor of Cultural Studies at Middlesex University. She is the author of *Fear of the Dark; Race, Gender and Sexuality in the Cinema*, published by Routledge in 1996.

I'm not an economist but ...

I was at a conference just recently, a weekend working gathering of folk on the left, and drawn from a variety of intellectual backgrounds. Up for discussion was a wide range of political issues. Among other things we addressed changing notions of identity (national, ethnic, personal), the challenges of the emerging forms of technological and organisational change, the form of politics embodied in 'the third way' ... and we discussed economic issues.

Most people took part in most discussions. Economists, those who were interested, felt quite able to join in a debate on 'cool Britannia', for instance. Yet in the discussions of 'the economy' most of those who had the courage to intervene, but who did not have formal economics training, felt it necessary to preface their remarks by an apology, or perhaps it was an explanation for the potentially uninformed nature of the question which was to follow : 'I'm not an economist but I'd just like to ask ...'

It seems to me that it is the brief of a journal like *Soundings* to open up to question some of the things that political discussions often take for granted. I would argue that the status and nature of economics is one of those things.

Way back in the dark days after Margaret Thatcher's first election victory Keith Joseph, then in his pomp as Secretary for Education, prompted a change of name for one of the country's leading grant-giving bodies, whose function was to fund social and economic research. It had until then been quite happily known as the Social Science Research Council. Sir Keith, however, believed this nomenclature seriously to misrepresent the situation, and after debate and counter-argument, the name was changed to the Economic and Social Research

Council. Two highly significant points were being made in this change. First, that most of these 'social' disciplines were not 'sciences' at all (and this was a point about quality and status; it was not being argued that 'social' disciplines were a different form of knowledge from, say, natural or physical sciences but of equal status; what was being argued was that they were inferior: they had not made the grade as proper sciences). Second, it was being argued that 'economics' had to be distinguished from this mushy social stuff. It is not explicit in the new title, but it is very definitely implicit that unlike the rest of the social sciences economics really is 'scientific'. The Economic and Social Research Council. The economic and the social were separated.[1]

N ow, this is a separation which cuts both ways. Not only does it, in Sir Keith's view of the world, relegate the study of the social to the outer darkness of non-science; it also removes from the idea of 'the economic' any notion that the economy is a social process too (and not, for instance a machine, or a law of nature). The effects on our understanding of both the 'social' and the 'economic' are disastrous.

And it seems to me now, as I reflect upon the goings-on at that recent conference, that in large parts of the left we have absorbed, and still cannot quite shake off, that same way of thinking.

Like the force of gravity?

To say that the economy is not a machine, nor the workings of the market equivalent to a force of nature, may seem to be stating the self-evident. Yet only recently Bill Clinton (and as we shall see the opinion is by no means confined to him) delivered himself of the observation that we can no more resist the current forces of economic globalisation (meant here in the narrow sense of the pressures towards free trade) than we can resist the force of gravity. Social processes are equated with 'laws of nature'. On the one hand, and perhaps more than anything for the sake of mischievousness, one might point out that this is a man who spends a good deal of his life flying about in aeroplanes, thus in this and other ways quite effectively resisting the force of gravity. On the other hand, and more seriously, this proposition was delivered to us by a man

---

1. They were separated in the title, that is. The ESRC in its actual practice, continues also to fund research which recognises the connections.

who has spent much of his recent career precisely trying to protect and promote this law of nature which is neo-liberal globalisation (his promotion of GATT, his support for the World Trade Organisation, his desire to speed up the signing and implementation of NAFTA). As far as I am aware, the law of gravity itself does not require politicians either to argue for it or to implement it.

And if (some) politicians think the economy (by which they mean the market, and the capitalist economy) is like a force of nature, some economists think it is like a machine. Alone among the sciences (both 'social' and 'natural') economics relies for its claims to scientific status on its likeness to nineteenth-century Newtonian mechanics. It is this which it takes as the basis of its claim to scientificity. This is in spite of the fact that it is now widely acknowledged that this is a false claim, that much of physics itself is no longer like that. Yet the claim is still made and still widely accepted.

This is, of course, already being challenged and perhaps most particularly by many an economist. The 'economics' to which I have been referring is perhaps better specified as a particular form of Anglo-Saxon neo-classical/neo-liberal economics; but there are many other approaches. The article by Sean Gray in this issue gives some intimation of debates within the discipline. The model is constantly challenged within its home discipline: it would be good to see an awareness of that challenge extend to the political arena.

Consequences

For the consequences in politics of having imbibed this way of thinking are considerable - and fundamental to political debate (and a kind of political impasse) at the moment.

First, and most obviously, it leads to the assumption that there is nothing we can do about the nature of the workings of the economy, whether internationally or through national economic policy. Clinton's invocation of the law of gravity may be an extreme formulation, but the general acceptance of the laws of the market (and hence of global finance, multinational corporations, and so forth), both as inevitable and as the only possible forms of economic mechanism, is fundamental to the whole structure of 'third way' politics. 'The economy' is taken as given. 'It' is doing things to which we must perforce adapt. There is no possibility, on this view of the world, of intervening in or moulding the character of the operation of the economy itself. This is evident in third way politics even at their most interventionist. Tony Blair's autumn thoughts on restraining the excesses of the international finance system were prefaced by the thought that we should not try to stop it doing what it is doing; we should merely try to prevent its perceived excesses. The excesses which are perceived, of course, are those which threaten to rock the boat of the big western economies and multinational capital. Excesses such as dramatically increasing global inequality, or the continuing desperation of mass malnutrition and lack of the most basic services are, from this vantage point, imperceptible. Within the country, too, New Labour operates largely by letting the economy do its thing and then correcting at the margins for its negative results. There is little attempt (though there is some - the minimum wage might come into this category) to prevent the generation of inequality in the first place. It is as though there were only one possible form of economic growth. And yet we know that there have been periods in which economic growth has taken place without producing the alarming inequalities which are so characteristic of today. Fundamentally, what is going on here is the autonomisation of the economic - the exclusion from political debate of the basic workings of the economy.

Second, this way of thinking of the economy as a perfectible machine is tied up with the idea that it is devoid of cultural or social content. It is this kind of view which underlies the breathtaking presumption that one can march, armed only with a formulaic model, into a country with the massive and deep social and cultural geography of Russia, and expect it to 'work'. (And then of course to blame Russia, rather than the presumption, for its self-evident failure.) It is this way of thinking which has provoked disagreements, for instance between Japan and the USA, within bodies such as the World Bank. It is this kind of scathing assumption that there is only one form, even of capitalism, which leads to the reduction of cultural variation to racist epithets such as 'cronyism'.

'The economy' itself is fully social and cultural. It has social and cultural causes and dimensions as well as outcomes. Economic pronouncements are not pronouncements of some indisputable 'truth' but discourses like anything else, and fully analysable and disputable as such. We may have shed demands for the nationalisation of the commanding heights and so forth, but that doesn't mean there is only one way to run an economy. It is high time the economic was brought back within the realm of the politically contestable.

DM

Tony Blair and the jargon of modernisation

Alan Finlayson

Alan Finlayson *scrutinises the contradictions and political implications inside the New Labour rhetoric of modernisation.*

> Modernisation is not an end in itself. It is for a purpose. Modernisation is not the enemy of justice but its ally.
>
> Tony Blair, Labour Party Annual Conference 1997

The jargon and rhetoric of 'modernisation' abound within the discourse of the current Labour government. It is a rhetoric that is central to the vision, or 'project' of 'New Labour'. But what does it mean?

A number of competing interpretations of the New Labour phenomenon have considered the meaning of 'modernisation' but they do not always focus on it as a term fulfilling a particular rhetorical and ideological function. For example, modernisation has been taken to be: the name of the process whereby the Labour Party adopts a Thatcherite agenda; a continuation, perhaps culmination, of the party reforms first attempted by Gaitskell; simply an empty term hiding the single sin of having nothing to say.

Mike Kenny and Martin Smith argue that interpretations of Blair such as these underestimate both the novelty of his political approach and the complexity of forces, structural and ideological, to which it is a response. Frustratingly, however, while advocating a 'multi-dimensional interpretative framework' that can be sensitive to the discontinuities and contradictions that mark any long-term process of ideological change, they have yet to specify the procedure through which such an analysis may be undertaken or what conclusions it might lead to. They do, though, make the important point that Blair's ideological position represents more than just a capitulation to Thatcherism or the victory of a 'labourist' accommodation with capital. Rather, they argue, it entails the attempt to change 'the party's instincts and values in accordance with this new political economy'.[1]

It is my intention here to try and 'get at' what Blair and New Labour represent, in the context of this attempt to change values in line with a perceived new politico-economic reality, by homing in on the term 'modernisation'. Thinking about the uses of the term modernisation may help expose some of the underlying conceptions of 'Blairism' and the way it conceives of contemporary political change. It is not my intention to unmask a single, true meaning of modernisation or Blairism. Rather, I aim to show that a number of themes converge on this term and that, while some may have perfectly sound implications, it is also possible that without clear thought, they may become the basis for a continuing capitulation to the Thatcherite legacy. Blair's is a political project in the process of being defined. What that project comes to mean will in part depend on how 'modernisation' is conceived. Michael Rustin argued in a recent issue of *Soundings*:

> It is a notable and defining fact about 'New Labour' that for the first time the power of capital and the markets which empower it is regarded as merely a fact of life, a reality to be accommodated to, and not a problem, force to be questioned and resisted. The abstractions of 'globalisation', 'individualisation', even 'informationalism', can be used to reify the real agents and interests which dominate the contemporary world (Editorial, *Soundings* 8).

The extent of such reification is related to the meanings given to the concept of 'modernisation'. It is potentially what this concept both reflects and produces since, as we shall see, it tends to locate such processes of 'globalisation',

---

1. Mike Kenny and Martin Smith, '(Mis)understanding Blair', *Political Quarterly*, Vol.68, No.3, 1997, p229.

'informationalism' (often simplistically understood and uncritically interpreted) in the exigencies of a social and historical development conceived as given.

We will take the following steps: firstly we will examine some actual uses of the term in Blair's own rhetoric; we will then begin to see that the concept of modernisation carries with it certain connotations that are manifest in the Blair project, particularly a brand of celebratory patriotism; next, we will briefly consider some of the origins of the term 'modernisation'. In so doing it will become clearer that the idea of modernisation contains within it a latent theory of historical development that leads to a philosophy of given cause. This recognition will enable us to focus on the connection between the rhetoric of modernisation and the idea of the nation as the necessary form of abstract community that must follow a route through history. It is around this that Blairite notions of civic responsibility are supposed to cohere. These two implications of the term 'modernisation', a philosophy of given cause and an attachment to nation, profoundly shape and define, sometimes in contradictory fashion, the ideology of Blairism.

Tony Blair's rhetoric of modernisation

The speeches of Tony Blair are a good place to start tracing the logic behind 'modernisation'. It may be argued that since set-piece speeches are constructed moments of rhetoric they can reveal only the surface gloss a politician wishes to display and obscure that which they really think. But it is their status as rhetoric that makes such speeches useful for the present analysis. These set-pieces are precisely about the 'vision' a politician wishes to express, the broad brush picture within which they may encapsulate their intentions. It is this vision on which an appeal is believed to rest and which shapes the kinds of long term policy strategy they construct.

Blair's speeches abound with references to the 'modern' party, his 'modern' vision and the newness of this 'modern' world. The first speech Blair gave to the party conference after being elected Prime Minister was quite clear in terms of this general vision. He wanted Britain to be 'nothing less than the model 21st century nation ... ' the construction of which depends on 'drawing deep into the richness of the British character ... old British values but a new British confidence'.[2] This appeal to the nation is not unique to

2. Tony Blair, Speech to Labour Party Conference, Brighton 1997, p1. Here after *LP97*. Other conference speeches are referred to as *LP95, LP96* etc. All page numbers are from texts issued by the Labour Party's media office at the relevant conference

Blair and can be found in the rhetoric of most party leaders be they Labour or Conservative. There are obvious reasons why politicians in a given nation state should base their rhetoric on an appeal to that nation. However, this is also a way in which an ideological project can achieve an appearance of legitimacy. Finding itself rooted in the given history, traditions and character of the national people, a political project can present itself as simply operating in conformity with that people. Thatcherism certainly utilised a discourse of nation in this way. Blair gives it a populist twist almost speaking as if the nation is newly freed from a colonial yoke. He speaks of people being 'liberated', of government returned to the people. This people is the bearer of the project: to return to his 1997 conference speech, he spoke of 'a quiet revolution now taking place. Led by the real modernisers - the British people' (*LP97*, p6).

The depth of this connection between modernisation and nationhood is something to which we shall shortly return. For the moment it is enough to recognise the importance of this stress on the modernising impulse of the British people. To legitimise modernisation as a political project, Blair seeks to locate the impetus for it, not in a cadre of political élites, but in the British people themselves. Thus any potential conservative argument that reform necessarily foists unwarranted change on the nation is trumped in advance by the construction of a story where change, renewal and modernisation are intrinsic to the tradition of the nation. Hence:

> From the Magna Carta to the first parliament to the industrial revolution to an empire that covered the world; most of the great inventions of modern times with Britain stamped on them: the telephone; the television; the computer; penicillin; the hovercraft; radar ... change is in the blood and bones of the British - we are by our nature and tradition innovators, adventurers, pioneers (*LP97*, p7).

In this conference speech Blair's claim was followed by a highly apposite quotation from Milton who was described as 'our great poet of renewal and recovery'. It is a description of England, taken from *Areopagitica*: 'a nation not slow or dull, but of quick, ingenious and piercing spirit, acute to invent, subtle and sinewy of discourse, not beneath the reach of any point that human capacity can soar to'.

The lines that follow those quoted by Blair could perhaps be seen as encapsulating his vision: 'methinks I see in my mind a noble and puissant nation rousing herself like a strong man after sleep and shaking her invincible locks' (*LP97*, p7). The moment of the Miltonian intervention is particularly interesting in this context. It marked an opening sally in what would become the defining radical struggle of English history - and the period most debated by historians interested in the modernisation of Britain. That Blair should, however unconsciously, identify his project with that of one of the most epochal moments in British history is surely instructive. The upheavals and conflicts of seventeenth century England fostered a strengthened sense of particularity and identity and engendered crucial developments in the deployment of national consciousness. In such development the notion of Englishness was always related to a wider political philosophy.

Blair's rhetoric works in a similar way, seeking to arrange itself on the side of the nation, opposing the anti-national interests in the establishment. As he put it in his 1994 conference speech: 'the new establishment is not a meritocracy but a power élite of money-shifters, middlemen and speculators ... people whose self-interest will always come before the national or the public interest' (*LP94*, p160). In contrast, Blairism will transform the nation or rather assist the nation to transform itself. As Kenny and Smith point out, Blair's attachments to conservative moral traditions (law and order, community, family and so forth) 'fit neatly with his attempt to reclaim an aggressively patriotic version of English nationalism for Labour and his repeated deployment of the "one nation" label' (p221). However Blair doesn't simply move onto the terrain of conservative patriotism. He reshapes that terrain making it appear fit for the 'challenge' of modernisation. Thus the country must draw on its deep character, exploiting the fact that the nation is one with:

> proud democratic traditions ... of tolerance, innovation and creativity ... an
> innate sense of fair play ... a great history and culture. And when great challenges
> face us, as they have twice this century, we rise to them. But if we have a fault, it is
> that unless roused, we tend to let things be. We say 'things could be worse'
> rather than 'things should be better'. And the Tories encourage this fault; they
> thrive on our complacency. I say it is time we were roused (*LP94*, p23).

The country will be roused for a project of 'national renewal' ready to face the new world and embrace change. This is a battle of national historical significance, a battle for the soul of that nation to return it to its true inheritance, modernised and 'free to excel once more' (*LP97*, p7).

There is no denying a certain radicalism in this discourse, although its roots in notions of Englishness may be questionable from a wider, British, viewpoint. This radicalism, though, is perhaps blunted by the way modernisation is fitted into a story about British history and the processes required for the continuation of its particular narrative. These processes are partly matters of political economy, but also technology: 'We know what makes a successful creative economy. Educate the people. Manage the country's finances well. Encourage business and enterprise. But each bit requires us to modernise and take the hard choices to do it ... We have been a mercantile power. An industrial power. Now we must be the new power of the information age' (*LP97*, p8). Indeed, we 'face the challenge of a world with its finger on the fast forward button; where every part of the picture of our life is changing' (*LP97*, p7).

Modernisation appears to refer to a large scale sense of change, development and transformation, something different to what has come before. It also seems to mean something specific to do with new technology (especially new technology) and information superhighways, a shift in mode of production from steam and electricity to computer technology (post-Fordism in other words), women in the labour force and so forth. But modernisation also covers more generalised trends in government action. In terms of specific policies it seems to refer to the necessary changes required in most areas of state action. We need skills, talents and education 'and every single part of our schools system must be modernised to achieve it' (*LP97*, p8). Here modernisation refers both to the deployment of new forms of technology and facing up to the demands of such technology. We need smaller class sizes, and expanded nursery education: 'the money will be there but in return hard choices and modernisation' (*LP97*, p9). These hard choices include taking over failing schools and LEAs and sacking poor teachers. But bear in mind that these hard choices are forced on us by the imperative of modernisation which in turn derives from the inexorable progress of our island story. There is no alternative: 'The hard choice: stay as we are and decline. Or modernise and win'(*LP97*, p10).

The NHS, 'the greatest act of modernisation any Labour Government ever did' (*LP97*, p13), similarly requires adaptation. As with schools there will not simply be more money since 'the NHS itself needs modernisation and hard choices' (*LP97*, p13). Perhaps the 'clearest' statement of what modernisation entails is this:

> I say to the country in all honesty. You can have the education revolution, the health revolution, the welfare revolution. But it means hard choices. It means us all getting involved. And it means modernisation (*LP97*, p14).

Modernisation means everything we have to do and we have to do what we do in order to be modernised. The hard choices it entails are encapsulated in an 'enlightened patriotism' that is the shell from which modernisation will emerge. The principles of Labour are the principles of Britain, there must be a 'supreme national effort' which will be 'held together by our values and by the strength of our character', our nature as 'a giving people' (LP97, p19). We will be a beacon to the world if the people 'unite behind our mission to modernise the country' (*LP97*, p20).

The sensibility and outlook that informs this perspective can be found in all of Blair's conference speeches as party leader. These texts are remarkable for their consistency of vision, employing the same phrases and examples. In 1994 it was 'time to break out of the past and break through with a clear and radical and modern vision for Britain. Today's politics is about the search for security in a changing world.' Here too, the stress was on new technology and the changes it will force on occupational structure and the labour market (*LP94*, pp11-12).

At the 1995 conference Blair told us about 'a new age to be led by a new generation', the popular culture generation of colour TV, Coronation Street and the Beatles (*LP95*, p4-5). The problem was that 'we live in a new age but in an old country', hanging on to an antiquated class system that needs to prepare to win the 'knowledge race'. All of this related to promises to bring the information superhighway to every school, library and, eventually home (*LP95*, p6-7). The modernising of public services via new technology was called for as was constitutional reform to be carried out by the 'patriotic party'(*LP95*, p17). By 1996 Blair was speaking of 1000 days for 1000 years, declaring this the 'Age of Achievement', globalisation, education, education and education, all of which again related primarily to new computer technology (*LP96*, p1). The age of achievement stands against the age of decline, drawing on an intrinsic 'national ethos and spirit' such that Labour will be 'part of the broad movement of human progress'. This movement links Blair's party with, extraordinarily, the Old Testament prophets, Wilberforce, and the Union movement. Carried away with his own version of Miltonian rhetoric, Blair speaks of the nation's intrinsic 'common sense', historic institutions, 1000 years of history and declares that the party is 'not just turning a page in history, but writing a new book. Building the greatness of our nation through the greatness of its people ... let us call our nation to its destiny' (*LP96*, p14). Thus, plugged into the world wide web, paradise is regained.

We can identify three main strands to the analysis thus far. Firstly, we can see the wide application of the term modernisation to encompass and define everything that is held to be good and necessary. It refers to everything Blairism stands for and represents nothing less than a projected attempt at national renewal and transformation centring on new technology, global markets and the so-called skills revolution. Whatever it is that the British education system and health service require can be called 'modernisation'. This broad deployment of the term necessarily entails the antagonist against which modernisation can be distinguished, so establishing for it some stability of signification. Hence the concept is defined, in part, by its opposition to a hypothesised anti-modernisation that must be excised from the Labour Party but is also incarnated in the failed Tory Party. The preponderance of a crude dualism between old and new in current political discourse testifies to this process. That which is not 'on-side' or 'on-message' is by definition anti-modernisation and out-dated. In this way 'modernisation' is a key trope for New Labour and Blairite rhetoric anchoring an ideological operation, working to include that which is pre-defined as part of the project and securing that project's unity by excluding everything opposed to it as part of a history that has been surpassed. To some extent this is a necessary aspect of any major political project. However, in drawing such lines the danger is that of rendering equivalent otherwise diverse opinions and schools of thought. It reduces to a neat and enclosed binary opposition a rich and diverse source of political ideas. And, as we shall see, it also obscures the fact that New Labour is very dependent on some very old left ideas that are modernist, if not modern, and definitely unfashionable.

Secondly we must note the frequent conjunction of modernisation with exhortations structured around a vision of the nation. Modernisation is in accordance with the historic and innate sense of the British people, the logical extension of all that Britain has ever done. Here, the nation appears simultaneously as one in need of modernisation and one that is already, of itself, engaging in the process. It requires only that the nation be roused from its slumbers and revolutionised so it can face up to hard choices that it must accept or die - hard choices foisted on us by the inexorable march of human progress but lived up to by this Christian world-historical movement. Modernisation thus emerges as a given, legitimated both by its inevitability and by being located within the very character of the nation. We shall return to this.

'Modernisation has a respectability with the left, not least because it sounds progressive'

Thirdly, we can begin to see how the blanket use of the term furthers an impression of inevitability and necessity. Forces are at work bringing about the need for modernisation. Such forces are inevitable and clearly definable - technological transformation, the 'obvious' failure of the social-democratic welfare state, globalisation and so forth. Since such forces are irreversible the political challenge becomes construed as one of living up to these forces rather than assessing them and deciding how politics should respond to them. This further means that specific reforms to core state services, such as education and health, can be justified on the basis of their *a priori* (and unquestionable) necessity rather than on the basis of whether or not they make sense and achieve some stated end other than merely being in accord with forces beyond our control.

All of this makes for a profoundly anti-political outlook. It reduces politics to the management of state and society in the interests of a given, even algorithmic, world economy. Political actions become justified as the result of the inevitable pressures of this irreversible economic logic. As Chantal Mouffe has noted: 'The usual justification for the "there is no alternative" dogma is globalisation ... This kind of argument takes for granted the ideological terrain which has been established as a result of years of neo-liberal hegemony and transforms what is a conjunctural state of affairs into an historical necessity' (Chantal Mouffe, *Soundings* 9).

Similarly, Doreen Massey points out that the term 'globalisation' has become a 'de-politicised, unexamined, assumption', spoken of as if it is a given, inevitable, process and in such generalisable terms that its 'politico-economic specificity' is obscured. Globalisation is a politically motivated *neo-liberal* globalisation but is treated as if it is a *deus-ex-machina* to which we had just better get used to.[3]

However, globalisation and modernisation are not inter-changeable and it is noticeable that it is the latter that, so far, dominates Blairite rhetoric. While clearly often informed by a crude globalisation thesis Blairites speak of modernisation more often. This, I suggest, is because the term has a respectability with the left, not least because it sounds progressive, but also because it has a history in the thinking of the British Left and in the Labour Party. Modernisation is part of our tradition. It is to this we now turn.

The origins of modernisation

The idea of modernisation has long been a part of the intellectual tool box of the British Labour Party, not least since Crosland. However it would be a mistake to think that it can mean the same now as it has in the past. Blair and New Labour's use of the term contributes to a reshaping of its implications at the same time as that use is shaped by the term's history. There is not space here to undertake anything like a full genealogy of 'modernisation' but there are clearly some key moments.

The 'problematic' of modernisation has marked theories and analyses of the British state, society and economy for a long time. The left variant of this analysis crystallised in the celebrated Anderson/Nairn theses: the argument that '1688' and all that represented an incomplete, possibly 'premature', bourgeois revolution. By not having a 'proper' revolution Britain failed to eradicate the feudal legacy, leading to a compromise arrangement where new structures of capital co-existed with an archaic 'superstructure' encompassing aristocratic traditionalism and unable to embrace the necessary processes of 'rationalisation' to develop a fully modern state form.

From this perspective, the British state is understood as incompletely modernised (where modernisation is in some sense a necessary and 'normal' path of development) and new political projects can be analysed in terms of how they match up to the demands of modernising Britain. The Wilson and

---

3. Doreen Massey, 'Problems with Globalisation', Editorial, *Soundings* 7.

Heath governments, for example, could be interpreted in terms of failed attempts at bringing about modernisation. Is it possible that, in some measure, the Blair project conceives itself as modernisation on this scale?

That this perspective does influence Blairism is incontestable, for it is part of the intellectual landscape of most of the British left. It informs the analysis of Will Hutton, for example, and was a key point for analyses of Thatcherism developed by important writers such as Andrew Gamble and Stuart Hall. In particular, modernisation formed an underlying theme to the perspectives developed in the 1980s in the pages of *Marxism Today*. Theories of British decline were predicated on variants of the Anderson-Nairn theses and from them emerged the view that Britain required something called modernisation and that Thatcherism was to be understood as a failed attempt at 'regressive-modernisation'. Thus in 1987, for example, Eric Hobsbawm, in *Marxism Today*, called for Labour to establish a coalition of interests dedicated to bringing about modernisation of the British economy. 'Labour will return to office only as a party which offers such a New Deal: modernisation - and in a human and responsible manner. Whatever the long-term prospects for Britain, what the country needs now for any kind of future is such a transformation.'[4] This entailed accepting some of the Thatcherite reforms and accepting that Labour should be ready to 'disrupt old habits and practices'. Hobsbawm also called for a combination of market and state planning that would enable a socially responsible modernisation incorporating a commitment to social justice. It is easy to see this sort of argument reflected in contemporary New Labour.

The *Marxism Today* analysis, inasmuch as it ever amounted to a single coherent view, was underpinned by a reasonably weighty theoretical approach and a recognition that Thatcherism was a strategic political project aiming to realign the balance of forces in the state and economy and establish a new hegemonic consensus. The prescription was the organisation of a counter-hegemonic project binding together social groups into an alliance that would certainly represent some sort of modernising force but would do so in order to respond to and direct economic forces and changes towards goals of equity, autonomy, democracy and social justice. One cannot doubt that this still informs, in some way, the theories of Labour policy makers. One can doubt,

---

4. Eric Hobsbawm, 'Out of the Wilderness', *Marxism Today*, October 1987, p17.

though, the extent to which the implications of the *Marxism Today* analysis were fully understood.

Modernisation in *Marxism Today* was the name of a political project (not an economic process) that would modernise in order to unite a broad coalition of interests and secure a new hegemony. The impression given by the current Labour rhetoric of modernisation is that it is the name of a single impersonal process to which political projects are subordinate. The distinction is crucial. The former regards modernisation as something to be achieved, shaped by the strategic use of the state as an educative instrument (in the singular Gramscian rather than Blairite triplicate sense). But New Labour regards modernisation as something independent of politics and as an inevitable process. The state can only be used to enhance competitiveness and make the country fit for participation in the new world.

The danger of this mutation in left thinking was always implicit within the Anderson-Nairn theses. That perspective tended to treat the form of the state in Britain as an invariable given. It can be too easy to think as if the British state, at some fundamental level, hasn't really changed since the 1688 'settlement'. This constitutes the state structure itself as the problem and downplays the need to address the impact differing political strategies and ideologies have had. From such a perspective the state is conceived in very narrow terms as a set of constitutional structures and procedures. All one has to do is establish the correct formula for 'modernising' it and then apply it while damning all criticism of the true way as pre-modern and out of touch with reality. This, of course, is what New Labour is doing.

It is not my intention to simply reject all the analyses of Hutton, *Marxism Today* or indeed all the ideas informing the present government. Rather, it is to stress the irreducibly political nature of the state and of strategies oriented towards re-ordering that state. Such strategies cannot follow a pre-ordained recipe since they are ongoing political processes. The state we are in is not simply the result of ancient historical exceptionalism. It is a state shaped by the political strategies of the past. It is a Thatcherite state and can only be re-shaped when this is recognised and surpassed.

The danger is that modernisation will be subordinated to other discourses with purchase on the term. Not the least of these is the new neo-liberal orthodoxy that is sustained by the Clintonite strategy of 'triangulation' and seeks only to conform to perceived shifts in the electorate and economy. Subject to discourses of modernisation of this sort, that which is contingent is transformed into the necessary. Economic policy is 'de-politicised' as it becomes a matter of inevitability. Modernisation comes to mean subordination to a set of assumptions about economic development rather than the shaping of present conditions to contribute to a social good. The rhetoric of modernisation both marks these tendencies in New Labour ideology and helps to produce them. It contains within it implications of a deterministic kind but also, in being a term with a specific history in the British Labour Party, helps to anchor the discourse, to some extent, within the traditions of that party. The critical question is whether modernisation is uttered in the language of the labour movement, the language of Marxist history, the language of neo-liberal economic orthodoxy or a new language invented by Tony Blair and advisers. It seems likely that it comes from all of these, enabling the modernising project to appeal to a variety of political, economic and intellectual constituencies. Whether or not it ultimately means the success of neo-liberal paradigms is perhaps still an open question. As Dennis Potter once commented 'the trouble with words is you don't know whose mouths they've been in.' And without scrutiny of where a word like 'modernisation' has been and how it is being used, intellectual associates of New Labour may find themselves losing their voice.

Modernisation and nationalism

We have already made mention of another, broader, archaeology underneath the term 'modernisation' that requires our attention. Its reference is not confined to the development and decline of the British state and economy since 1688 nor to contemporary strategic political disputes over perceived globalisation. The very idea of modernising, of becoming more modern, implies certain assumptions about the process of history as a particular sort of linear progression. It is in this sense that modernisation finds itself closely allied to the idea of the nation.

The association between nationalism and the sociological notion of modernisation is well attested to in scholarship of the phenomenon. For Marxist and liberal historians alike, the nation (and being a nation state) is understood as a hallmark of modernity. The nation defines the abstract form of community that predominates in the industrialised world to such an extent that, as post-colonial theorists from India to Ireland have argued, it comes to appear as if, to be modern, one must first pass through the necessary stage of acquiring nationhood.

The 'imagining' of national community derives from and entails notions of modernisation and combines within it a very specific sense of time, history and space. As Benedict Anderson argues, to imagine the nation is to imagine a large collective of people all occupying the same time and space: 'the idea of a sociological organism moving calendrically through homogenous empty time is a precise analogue of the idea of the nation, which is also conceived as a solid community moving steadily down (or up) history.'[5] To imagine the nation means also to imagine a particular, and modern, notion of history as a sequence of causally related events moving in some direction. And the reverse is also true. To imagine time, or history, in that way means also to imagine the vehicle that moves in and through that history. The vehicle which has been bequeathed to us is the nation.

'Modernisation', for New Labour, implies just such a notion of history in terms of some sort of progressive development driven by some sort of external force. Hence the frequent connection of modernisation with the nation. As the nation is the body subject to the forces of modernisation it is this which must be reconceived and rebranded and it is in it we must find the already written path to the pre-ordained future. Hence a concern with Britishness and, as we have seen, with locating Blairism in the given characteristics of that nation. This perhaps accounts in part for New Labour's tendency to celebrate very particular aspects of current popular culture in Britain and for the ease with which the death of Diana could be incorporated into the mission.

In the case of Blair's nationalist rhetoric, a rhetoric necessarily in conjunction with that of modernisation, the intention is to establish as already there that which is needed to legitimate the proposed 'change'. Such an ideological manoeuvre is far from unique to Blair and New Labour but it holds unique dangers. Not the least of these is the situation of such discourse in a state always made up of different national identities (and one more than a little contrary region) at a time of much vaunted devolution. There are contradictions between this attempt to mobilise a notion (essentially London-centric) of Britishness when Scotland and Wales are finally getting recognition for themselves.

In employing patriotic and nationalistic rhetoric Blair presents his approach as in the interest of the British people because it is already

---

5. Benedict Anderson, *Imagined Communities*, 2nd edn, Verso, London 1993, p26.

coincident with their core characteristics. The circularity between this definition of the nation and the pre-defined facts of modernisation can potentially act to exclude those who do not fit either. A party that sees itself as in charge of a historically pre-defined national mission is prone to underestimating the complex nature of the cultural transformation it is demanding and the extent to which it requires assistance from those outside the party's charmed circle. Furthermore, outside of international football competitions and the death of royals it is not at all certain that a rhetoric of nationhood even carries much force. In established nation states the rhetoric of nation is always about leaving things in place rather than uprooting them, at most encouraging only 'reform in order to conserve'.

But the prime danger with this populist patriotism is that it closes the loop with the rhetoric of modernisation. It renders change a matter of inevitability, a pre-established given, rather than something to be achieved. It is dictated by the forces of global production which must work in harmony with the nation since the nation is now defined as ... that which seeks to work in harmony with the forces of global production. Thus, Blair's populism further de-politicises an accommodation to contingent economic and political forces. Perhaps most sadly, given the probably good intentions of many in New Labour, such a process acts entirely against the reinvigoration of civic and public life. Why have a civic life if change is a matter of economic inevitability that is *a priori* and in harmony with the people? Anyone who whines about this just isn't one of 'the people'. We are, I think, familiar with this sort of thinking. It is part of Blair's inheritance from an 'old' left.

Conclusion

The rhetoric of modernisation can be seen to function as a way of drawing antagonistic lines of exclusion and inclusion. On one side is that which is modernised or attuned to modernisation and this is always good (if sometimes requiring a 'hard choice'). The other side is always, by definition, out of touch and anti-modernisation. Any institution or practice that is perceived as not working perfectly is held to require 'modernisation'. From this there inevitably follows the necessity of this thing called modernisation and the call for a new way that claims merit from recognising this supposed historical exigency and conforming to it. In a peculiar sense this aspect of the Blair project follows a certain vulgar Marxist tendency in that it regards itself as in line with a given logic external to its own political interventions.

The danger here is that rather than an opening up or broadening out of political thought, action and the constituencies drawn into politics, modernising New Labour will bring about a major narrowing - it is open to anyone so long as they accept the inevitability of a particular logic of social and economic development. The logic is one of submitting to trends and forces not assessing them and shaping them to go where we want them to. While reforms appear to be about opening things up to more flexibility and choice, tailoring what is offered to suit the multifarious needs of the unemployed, sick, disabled and so forth, they will not entail any opening up or extension of democracy if they are motivated by the desire to conform to a narrow logic. The choice offered will end up as that between accepting the inevitable or being given up on - no choice at all.

The rhetoric of modernisation may contain a drive for closure and enforced unity rather than diversity. People will be forced to change in order to satisfy the presumed needs of an economy fetishised as an independent force rather than the economy being shaped to fit whatever people decide are their needs. Flexibility of welfare will be about making us lean and hungry for global competition, not about being open-ended, diverse and democratic. Part of the achievement of Thatcherism was a 'de-politicisation' of the economy in order to present it as something to which we should live up to. This tendency is being furthered by the rhetoric of modernisation. In this context Blair's nationalist rhetoric closes the space even further, seeking to find the motor for such change already in place in the intrinsic characteristics of the nation when it was precisely these characteristics that the Anderson-Nairn thesis sought to critique.

If Blairism is not to be a way of recycling and re-presenting the neo-liberal consensus (because it doesn't engage rigorously and intellectually with the thought of neo-liberalism, seeking merely to bolt on some sort of ill-defined communitarian perspective) then it is exceptionally important to critically assess the rhetoric of modernisation. If New Labour hasn't broken with the Thatcherite settlement then the 'choice' and 'open-ness' it promises will be conceived in market terms. Freedom or autonomy will continue to be understood as equivalent to the extension of consumer based choice. If freedom and autonomy are to be thought through properly then we must break with market logic and think in terms of proper participation predicated on some notion of civic (and hence collective) engagement. This of course demands that those excluded be included - economically, socially and politically. In short equality has to be part of the agenda, indeed has to be part of 'modernisation' contrasted with the archaism of increasing poverty and widening gulfs of inequality.

We are not in some new space and time given to us by the generous motor of history. We are embedded within the Thatcherite restructuring of state and society - part of the 'momentous changes' that are upon us are the result of Thatcherite political actions not merely the result of impersonal economic or historical forces. The contemporary challenge is, in short, to be political at all: to conceive of state and society as political arrangements which require a deep rooted democratic culture of participation in order to shape, as far as possible, the future we think we might like to live in. The rhetoric of modernisation, with attendant themes of globalisation and nationalism, seeks to find change already upon us and directing us. It forgets that, although we do it in limited circumstances, it is 'we' who make history.

Scenes

Will Forrest

Alfred Ward Adult Admission Behavioural Unit, St Mary's Hospital

... Dayroom

The abscess in my bottom hurts. Their needle has punctured it again, and now my corduroys are wet with infected blood. I close my eyes; drug induced sleep is calling. Bland faces are haunting me; grandmother, aunt, brother; their features lost. I do not want to see these faces empty! What do I have to cling to now I cannot remember their smiles, their eyes?

Lloyd tugs at my arm. My heavy eyes open to find my hand being pulled towards him. He is holding me round my wrist, I let my muscles go, and he rubs the tip of his nose with the back of his hairy hand.

Heat. The central heating is on, the ventilation system broken, as it has been for many months. Lloyd's face is flushed, beads of sweat toppling over and running down through his side-burns leaving silver tracks. I feel wet. My pants are soggy from the bleeding abscess. It hurts.

Three rows of armchairs sit in disjointed lines, their sticky green covers ripped open, yellow foam bursting out. The windows are double-glazed with macrollon Perspex. No air can get in and the cloud of cigarette smoke hangs, trapped, in this day lounge. After each Hourly Points roll-call, when people find out if they have earned their cigarette or have failed and are going to Off Privileges, twenty fags are lit in here. The smoke is so thick my eyes burn and it's like looking through fog if I try to make out the other side of the room.

Derek is down the corridor in Off Privileges. He will be in there staring at bare walls for three days to reflect on his Sins. Three months ago he held up the dining room with a table knife. He tried to slash his throat which only left a red mark, it being a table knife, and when they approached him, he swore he was going to take one of them with him. They 'Control & Restrainted' him, rushing him with the dinner trolley and throwing a sheet over his head. They are trying to get him shipped to Broadmoor. It will be sad if they succeed. Derek has always been good to me, he speaks to me.

There is a thump from next door in the 'Quiet Room'. The Quiet Room is a strange name for that cell. It is bare and airless. Its only difference from the Off Privileges cell being that as well as being locked in there, you can lock yourself in voluntarily. The noise will be George, in on his self-imposed sentence. He will be sprawled over the battered, torn armchair for hours. Sometimes he masturbates in there and the nurses stand peering in through the observation window, sniggering. George goes about tapping people softly with his fist, which, I hear, is better than a few years ago when he used to hit. He locks himself in the Quiet Room to stop himself doing it and won't come out unless he is forced. If he taps somebody and runs into the Quiet Room they fight with him and drag him out of the Quiet Room into the cell of Off Privs. A bare cell is a bare cell. Their thinking, it's crazy.

Brian is shaking his head as he sits, hunched, in the front row of armchairs. He is choking on half formed cries, having one of his rare moments in reality. 'I'm a good boy', he says and wipes away a tear that is trickling down his rugged cheek, losing himself again in a less painful past when he went to a public school, played cricket, studied French. Most of the time he believes he is still there, rattling on, talking to people only he can see. Once in a while he will turn to somebody in the room and say, 'I am a good boy', and slap them on the back.

He stands up. With a leathery hand he brushes away another tear and strides across the room towards Andrew. Brian's trousers sag as he walks, looking as if they are about to fall to his knees. He does have a belt, tied tight, only he hasn't bothered to put it through the trouser-loops. Ash falls behind him like polluted snow. The butts collected in his lap spill onto to the carpeted floor. Brian reaches Andrew, who is slumped over two armchairs, and slams his hand on his shoulder. Andrew swings his feet off the chair, raising his fists.

None of us are supposed to put our feet on the furniture; it is 'poor social skills'. They will fail Andrew for that as well as for 'threatening behaviour' if they see this going on.

'Fuck off Brian!' Andrew swears, thin red veins appearing on his fat cheeks,

I was trying to fuckin' sleep.' His words gain length and volume, but realising that Brian won't take any notice he stands up and pushes him out of his way. Slipping on his shades he walks off into the games room, gut swinging.

'I am a good boy', Brian says, but there is no one in particular to hear. He looks down at his front. Vomit is smeared all over his jersey; a spread of colours with bits of chewed food stuck round the buttons. 'I'm a good boy,' he repeats apathetically.

The room is quiet. The sun has found a window and is shining through, hitting the smoke, and now the room is lost in a glistening mist. These drugs hurt, they make my head so numb that to think is a struggle. It is tempting just to sit and to stare. Cold. My eyes burn and I want to sleep. I am not allowed to during the day.

'Do it again, go on.'

Brian lopes from one foot to another, swinging his arm round in a bowling motion, the lights in his eyes bright for the second when the ball, if it were there, leaves his hand and charges, spinning, at the stumps.

Ash, butts, food, fall from his jumper. Trousers sagging, the split of his bottom showing, his elastic red underwear. 'I am a good boy Jack.' He wipes the worn folds of his face. 'I scored three goals against St Charles School for Boys – that's a hat-trick isn't it?'

Sniggers. Brian peers round at the nurses sitting about on the tatty armchairs, studying their smirks, watching them nudge each other. His trousers slip another notch. 'I'm a good boy, Jack.' He yanks his trousers up. They fall to his hips again.

'Do it again Brian, show Jane how you bowl!'

A small female nurse, bleached blond pony-tail bobbing, walks through the doorframe into the day area. She holds a 'staff' mug that steams into the smoke-filled dayroom. Jane leans against the wall near the others.

'I am a good boy, aren't I Jack?' He looks at Liam who gives him a thin smile, half-hidden by his ginger-brown moustache.

'You're a good boy Brian.'

Brian mimes his bowling skills again. In his mind a demonstration of his former glory, in theirs a freak performing for their fancy. Like in Victorian days. Anger wraps itself around my insides and squeezes tight as they laugh at him. School bullies. A crowd laughing at lepers because their own skin is untainted by disease. Easy to laugh in a pack at a man who has lost his own teeth, can't bite back. Jane takes a slurp of coffee.

Brian tried to kill himself when he was young. He's sixty now, admitted in the 1950s. They gave him ECT but he tried to kill himself again. I can still vaguely make out the scar on his neck between folds of loose almost jaundiced skin. Lobotomies were the in thing, so they gave him one. I can see the drill scars too, by his temples. Now he vomits over himself, can't stop talking, repeating school memories over and over again - all that is left of his dignity his upper class accent and the occasional parcel in the post, until his dad died two months ago.

'I am a big boy now, aren't I Jack?' He slaps Liam on the back, raises his voice, dentures dislodging. 'I am a big boy.'

'Brian.' Knocking Brian's hand off his shoulder Liam raises his eyes so he is looking Brian full in the face. 'What's the rules about touching?'

'I'm to keep my hands to myself, I'm a good boy Jack.' He twines his hands together as if trying to make himself small, slide out of view, as he turns to go.

'Give me a token Brian.'

'I'll change my jumper, I am a good boy.'

'Brian,' Liam's lips curl to a smile, a real smile this time, not a placating one to get his toy to play. 'Give me a token.'

'But I won't get a cigarette damn you Jack!' He backs away from Liam.

Cock fighting. Staff crowd round, standing in their lopsided, lazy stances. The dayroom's scarred armchairs bleeding yellow foam, the ripped poster on the wall they haven't bothered to take down, the Rampton designed notice-board listing Mental Health rights, stating reassuringly under which sections of the Mental Health Act it is your right to refuse: Psychosurgery.

'Give me a token Brian.'

His face goes grey. 'If you take my token, Jack, they won't give me a damn cigarette!' Brian stuffs his hand firmly into his trouser pocket where the tokens hide.

Liam grips Brian's wrist.

'That's two tokens Brian - give me them,' he squeezes, 'before it's three tokens and you lose your fag.'

'I am a good boy.'

I can see it coming. Next hour, he won't understand why he can't have his cigarette. Brian will try to explain that he had his tokens until 'some damn silly nurse' stole them from him, and that he wants his 'cigarette Jack!' Anger will blossom when he is told he can't have one without four tokens and he'll ask in desperation and confusion why they took them 'away then, damn Jack!'

They brain damaged him, now they're trying to teach the damaged matter that it's wrong to 'inappropriately touch' or to 'constantly talk when others are asking him to be quiet.' Dragged away to the Time Out room he'll bang and shout in the darkness against the cell door, still not understanding why they are locking him in, why they are doing this to him.

I don't either.

... Swimming

'Take him swimming.' Dave stands at the Quiet Room door as the needle and china cup are taken away.

Sweat. I had struggled with the nurses on the floor to get that mug, three nurses folding me in angled locks two feet away from the porcelain. Fighting. Fighting to break the china, leave them only my body to desensitise. Before my mind's eye lay another broken cup, another deep cut, this time slicing home, the jugular. Dave Heriot has had his play. The nurses he set to the task were tired, sweating. He had pulled down my jeans, sunk the clear fluid between the plunger and the tight sharp needle, into my infected potholed bottom.

Haloperidol is calling, that drugged up, dosed up, slip away feeling. The sleepy-numb, slowsome, brain malfunction sanctuary. But Dave's words, they penetrate my ears, creating a fear, a fear of a doped up man with a marathon to run. Fear of exhaustion. Scared of the aching, the gasping, of the collapse, rasps for air.

I close my eyes, curl into a ball on the hard concrete floor.

'Get him up.' He states, 'They're queuing, waiting to go.

Picking me up by my arms, keeping them in locks, they take me through to the airlock in front of Off Privs. My legs wobble. A saggy queue stands in the sea of cigarette burns on the green threadbare carpet. Skippy, six foot four, with a hanging head. He grins all the time. Lopes about gently with a soft grunt that he uses to answer everything. Skippy likes it here they say. Every time they move him back to a normal hospital he commits an attack so that he comes back. Last time he kicked a nurse in the balls so hard the guy had to have his testicles removed. Once he's here, though, he's the picture of placidity. A gentle giant with a friendly smile.

June, an elderly lady, sixty something, with a handbag and thick rimmed glasses, who always tidies everything, fighting the layers of fag ash with a disposable cloth. If she doesn't do gym they fail her for 'non participation', and she goes into solitary for a twenty-four hour target. Some of the nurses feel bad about it. Dave Heriot, charge nurse, says 'the ward programme applies to everybody.'

Andrew slumps against the doorframe with his beached-whale belly. George, Derek and Dyson. They stand with the hospital hand-out trunks in their hands.

Lloyd steps out of the office. Although he grips my wrists, he holds them kindly and looks at me softly with damp eyes. He is balding, over-weight, with an 'ello 'ello moustache.

'You all right?' He whispers.

I shake my head; his touch starts tears streaming. The medication is slip-sliding my brain.

Numb, I am escorted through the grounds on the internal road, past the flowerbeds and lawns that are immaculately shorn and pruned. We pass a bed of red Weeping Hearts in stony soil; it is their time to bloom. The delicate puffed flower, the teardrop that hangs below ...

The gym and café loom, a two-storey red-bricked building opposite the cricket pitch which the local cricket team plays on, patients kept out of their way. Same with the golf course. It's only for doctors and patients who pay, who are not on an health authority funded stay.

We step down the few wide steps and through the glass double doors, up a set of stone steps to the green doors of the changing rooms; one for 'girls' one for 'boys'. Their metal push-plates and symbols are moist with the condensation that is rolling out over us.

'Who's going in with 'im?' Taking me from Lloyd's arms, Liam points Lloyd, with an unfriendly gaze, towards the gallery, a small glass dock at the end of a short corridor from which you can watch the people in the pool. It has a lock so patients can't escape if they are to wait and watch the others in the baths. Everything here is escape-safe.

Heat. The changing room. Smelly socks. Water runs around the tile floor because the drains don't work so well. Men are everywhere, in the showers, dressing, or sitting wrapped in a towel on the wooden benches looking at us. The Alfred lot coming in.

'Okay, hurry up, get changed, out, out into the pool!' A lean mean machine, a firm man with small, tight orange trunks, dark complexion, dark eyes, dark hair. The gym instructor's gaze hits me.

'You going in with him Kurt?' Liam asks.

The gym instructor nods. 'Get your clothes off Will.' His army barracks background snaps loudly in his voice. I see him drilling new recruits in his bullies' paradise, till he left that job and used his skills for the fitness training of the mentally ill.

'Hurry up, hurry up, hurry up! I know your game,' he cocks his head as he looks at me undress. 'For every minute you waste it's an extra minute in the water. Hurry up!'

He smiles at Liam, pulls at the jumper I am struggling to take off. It rips. The tearing of cloth silences the changing room. Only for a second. The noise of human ablutions and voices switches back on.

Liam holds my trunks for me to step into. Naked I stand up, step into them. Feel him pull them and snap the waistband. Kurt pushes me through the de-verruca water onto the white prickle-tile poolside. He grabs my arm, marches me slowly round the sloppy edges to the deep end.

Red indoor kayaks rest against the wall at this end of the pool. Indoor canoeing is one of the things they use to attract nursing assistants to come, despite the poor pay. 'Facilities second to none' St Mary's say.

On the same wall as the kayaks, in an office that is built in the space that divides the pool from the gym, the other gym instructor peers through the open wooden door as he leans over a folder twiddling a pen round and round. A basketball hammers in the gym, bouncing, behind shouts and cries and a guy telling someone 'fuck you!'

Patients splashing about, the pool walls starting to echo with shouts and yells and the noise of breaking water. Kurt signals to Liam with a flick of his free hand. Liam stops leaning on the outside of the viewing bay glass and methodically paces round towards us.

He lays his hand on my shoulder, then pulls my arms behind my back, holding me while Kurt pulls down my trunks, yanking me out of them in front of the patients and staff. The female staff and female patients peer at my shrivelled balls.

'Can't have you swallowing your trunks now, can we?'

Pause. They push me into the deep end of the pool, shove. I smack the water with a slap and a sting of skin.

'Stay away from the sides!' shouts Liam. Jumping into the water Kurt stands where it laps round his neck as he stabilises himself with his arms.

I feel clothed by the water.

Treading water, I look at the clock on the wall at the far side. Medication, still numbing, blurs the numbers but I can see I have fifty minutes to go. Even then they'll not let it end, they'll make me tread water while the others jacuzzi and sauna and then get changed. No standing in the shallow end allowed, just my legs, arms, keeping me above the water.

It's a strange feeling, fearing and wanting to drown at the same time. The contradiction is only made possible by the overwhelming desire to rest, rest aching arms and hands, to stop kicking against the water. Despite the consequences I drift towards the shallower end. Hoping to sneak a rest on my toes, to ease my heaving breathing.

'Get back!!' shouts Kurt. He dives forward, his hand landing on my head as he pushes me under the water. Dunking, didn't get time to take a breath. Holding me under. I open my eyes and make out the orange colour of his shorts, his legs standing next to me. I can feel the weight of his body on my head holding me underneath. Thrashing, need to breathe, I am choking, can see the colour blue spreading down my arms as my veins rise. Need to breathe! He keeps holding me under. The water world grows hazy. Sensing the growing urgency of my struggling he lets go.

Air. As I thrash out of the water he pushes me back into the deep end. Air, but the aching of my muscles is still there. Gasping, I look at Lloyd. He stares helplessly from the bay. The clock. I still have another thirty-two minutes of this to go.

'Does he fuck want to die,' laughs Kurt to Liam. 'Bring him back tomorrow.'

Four Poems

Old Money

He changed my five
sixpences
for half a crown,
assumed I'd love
his bright idea,
its weight and size.
He smiled above
my doubts, held out
his open hand
and pocketed
my jingling five,
my perfect pile,
those spiral stairs.
The single coin
he pressed on me
was useless, gross,
it made me cry,
and in the end
he swapped them back,
shaking his head
making a face
that to my shame
though he's long dead
I don't forget.

Michael Laskey

Daughters of the house

Never again, never again!
but here they are again,
Sarah and Maggie, the door
scraping over the flagstones
and Mother shuffling across the landing.

And even after all this time
they line up jars of powdery prunes
biscuit tins sealed with rust
packets of custard powder and upstairs
behind the bars on the nursery windows
shake pillows, spread blankets.

If they could even begin to break out,
to wreck the kitchen, unroof the house,
imagine a heap of crumbling stone,
a bare patch of hillside, and under the nettles
a few broken tiles.

 But whenever they meet
'Remember?' says Maggie 'The time when.'
And they are walling themselves up again
locked together. 'The stone jam jars,' says Sarah,
'The egg crock, the meat safe.'

Their names scored in the plaster in the attic bedroom.
The stains in the larder.

Dorothy Nimmo

Somewhere Else

'Who is this man running with me, the shadow of whose hands I see?'
(*Song from the South-West*: Native American song)

I stare at paper and white snowfields
paint the mind.
You lived there, my father,
I know that behind the Great Light
your dreams shadow mine.

This man has always run with me.
He has your smile. His greying hair
frames my rising thoughts
and the snow falls and falls.

I shall lie and die in that snowfield,
where your spirit hunts mine.

Stephen Wade

Good person

The gods are weighing us, me
and my father. We sit on our twin pans and look
forwards into nothing, trying
to stay upright. He is
the heavier. They do this for our sake.

He has learned not to be wasteful.
He keeps crumbs.
He has been saving himself
in small pieces. Eyes front, he goes down
sedately. Surely they mean us no harm.

They incline their good faces – the very same
as in that childhood playground when I ran
to the seesaw, mounted, flew for a moment, and then
nothing, someone else sinking
through my skin, someone's blood on the beam.

Susan Wicks

Imagination without power

Notes on contemporary social movements in Italy

Mario Pianta

Mario Pianta *analyses civil society movements in Italy in the period following the collapse of activism in traditional left-wing parties and organisations.*

War in Bosnia, Serbia and Croatia, social collapse in Albania, the new crisis in Kosovo, a continuing flow of desperate immigrants from the southern shores of the Mediterranean: the list of recent foreign policy issues is also a list of the failures of Italian and European policy to prevent conflicts, develop new political and economic relations, integrate the Balkans and the Mediterranean into the broader European space. The same list, however, accounts for major campaigns developed by social movements in Italy. Far from the media highlights, 10,000 Italians have gone since 1993 to the countries of former Yugoslavia to bring aid and build peace and solidarity projects. The Italian Consortium of Solidarity, set up by the Peace Association, ARCI, and other groups, has 300 ongoing projects, mostly funded with grassroots fundraising, ranging from helping democratic organisations, to providing equipment to the Sarajevo independent tv station Channel 99, from social work to setting up local production of the goods so far provided by humanitarian aid programmes. At the end of July 1998 a solidarity day for Kosovo was organised, raising funds and collecting thousands of signatures under a petition for a peaceful solution to the conflict.

In Albania in the summer of 1997 representatives of 200 Italian organisations involved in solidarity work met, coordinating activities for rebuilding the country, including help to the Forum of Albanian NGOs, programmes of support to women and youth, and several solidarity projects.

In Italy, where the problem of Albanian refugees and illegal immigrants is a major one, efforts at providing hospitality and integration have come from Catholic church organisations such as Caritas, and hundreds of Albanian families have found homes and work thanks to the network set up by grassroots organisations.

Because immigration is emerging as a major social issue, left anti-racist organisations such as Neroenonsolo and the Anti-racist Network have slowly developed alongside the activity of many Catholic groups, albeit in this field a serious fragmentation of actions is evident and little widespread mobilisation emerges. A recent yearbook of anti-racist organisations, *Meticcia*, lists 100 groups: centres for hospitality, legal aid, multicultural education programmes and cultural activities all over the country.

Traditional solidarity work with Third World liberation movements has also been renewed with mass support for the Zapatistas in Mexico. Thousands of Italians have visited Chiapas in recent years, building solidarity projects and setting up programmes with local authorities and Italian institutions, as well as organising mass demonstrations in Rome. In June 1998 a hundred Italian observers, including several MPs and other international observers, visited the zones of conflict and broke the siege of the Mexican army on some Zapatista municipalities, bringing world attention to the repression in Chiapas.

International solidarity, humanitarian action, and the integration of immigrants are examples of the dynamism of Italian civil society in facing the new policy issues of the country and of Europe in ways which are more imaginative and effective than official policies of the centre-left government and of political parties.

Obviously, this does not mean that the fragmented social movements and grassroots groups are able to develop a comprehensive political vision for facing each of the new issues. Nor does it mean that the role of politics can be taken up by social action per se, *especially in a period when very little mass mobilisation exists. It simply means that social movements in Italy, although weaker in their mass base, still have the ability to understand the new issues as soon as they emerge, and act on them, developing sensible political positions, simple strategies, and providing the first concrete answers, however inadequate (relative to the vastness of the problems) they might be.*

Such social dynamism is all the more striking when it is contrasted with the inability of the centre-left Ulivo government coalition to pick up and turn into national policies any of the positive experiences developed in civil society. In the first two and a half years of its mandate the government has single-handedly pursued entry into the European Economic and Monetary Union, at the price of serious austerity programmes, and has hardly dealt with domestic social issues. The political system (left included) has focused on a series of constitutional engineering projects which ended in failure, has felt challenged by the investigations of magistrates after the Tangentopoli scandals, and has closed its ranks, increasingly distancing itself from society.

As a reaction to the power of organised crime, and its political protections, civil society has invented new ways to fight the mafia and organised crime, with the creation of *Libera*, a network of associations and personalities chaired by don Luigi Ciotti of the Gruppo Abele in Turin, one of the key players of solidarity work in Italy. *Libera* has given a nation-wide social perspective to the anti-mafia campaign, with a petition for taking over the assets of convicted mafia leaders and with educational programmes, while throughout Italy solidarity groups have emerged to help small shopkeepers and small business, and victims of organised crime and usury (which, believe it or not, has returned on a grand scale in this age of global finance).

Such actions in civil society have been of great value to the magistrates who are conducting bold investigations and trials against the mafia and its political protections. In contrast, again, political parties (left included) have been more worried about the political consequences of events such as the ongoing mafia trial of former Prime Ministers Giulio Andreotti (the most powerful figure of the old Democrazia Cristiana, in power for four decades) and

Silvio Berlusconi (the media magnate currently leader of the right-wing opposition and already condemned in bribery trials).

The main sector where experience of social movements has been massively turned into institutional politics is the environment. The arrival of the Greens in the government in the spring of 1996, with Edo Ronchi as Environment Minister, has been the culmination of a progressive entrance of personalities from the ecology movement into positions of power throughout Italian cities and regions, in political roles or as managers of local public enterprises dealing with energy, refuse collection or transport. At ENEL, the Italian energy public monopoly, the new president is Enrico Testa, a founder of Legambiente, a major environmental association and long-time opponent of nuclear power. While this has led to some improvements in environmental policies, the overall outcome of such experiences has still to be assessed.

Obviously such institutionalisation of the environmental movement has seriously weakened the capacity to mobilise of ecology groups, who are now mainly active on issues such as air pollution in cities, clean seas and protection of natural parks - all campaigns with little direct political visibility or impact.

What about the politics of work? With 12 per cent unemployment, Italian society is still confronted with a dramatic problem for two million people, mainly women and young people living in the South. And new jobs for the young mostly come in the form of temporary contracts with lower wages and no security, or as an external provision of services, collaborations and consultancies, in a rapidly spreading pattern of outsourcing work to self-employed individuals or very small companies.

In this context the three major Trade Unions - CGIL, CISL and UIL - still focus on the protection of the employed and of pensioners - as in the fierce confrontation with the government in the autumn of 1997. In contrast they pay little attention to the issues of new jobs and youth unemployment. In fact, trade unions have reacted with unease and hostility to the political deal obtained in late 1997 by Rifondazione Comunista - the left party supporting the coalition but remaining outside government responsibilities - to introduce legislation for a 35-hour week. While the law is to be voted by the autumn of 1998, little mobilisation has taken place on the perspective of a reduction of working time.

Unions still rely on a close corporatist pact with the government and Confindustria, the increasingly aggressive employers' organisation, but are themselves divided over longer-term strategy. CGIL, the left confederation, holds on to a traditional union strategy and the only novelty has been the organisation in 1998 of NIDIL, a new union for trying to organise the self-employed involved in the 'outsourcing economy'. CISL, the Catholic Union, on the other hand, aims to reorganise the representation of a broad range of centrist Catholic organisations active on social and work issues.

Outside the main trade unions, where an often lively internal debate can be found, with strong criticism from the left minority in CGIL, not much has been built on the issue of work. In recent years a number of Grassroots Union Committees (Cobas) have emerged on the extreme left and in some occupations (railway workers, some large firms, public employment), but they did not emerge as new key players in the campaigns for work. Little support has developed also for specific actions on unemployment such as the March for Work of 1998. Especially in cities, such as Naples, where the jobless problem is more dramatic, there are occasional bursts of protest by the unemployed, organised in grassroots groups with often confused political affiliations.

Rather than with trade union actions or political campaigns, Italian civil society has addressed the themes of the economy and of work by developing direct initiatives in the production and distribution of goods and services, building self-organised answers to the needs left unsatisfied by both the market and the state. A rapid growth of 'Third Sector' activities has taken place in the past five years: including social co-operatives which help to integrate disabled workers and immigrants and provide social services and care activities; associations and co-operatives which work on cultural issues (organising public events and training courses, running tours of museums, protecting the cultural heritage); and organisations involving sporting activities, youth exchanges

and environmental projects. A broad definition of the non-profit sector in Italy includes about 50,000 organisations, 418,000 employees and about 300,000 volunteers (both measured in full time equivalents).[1]

These diverse streams of the social economy, with either Catholic roots or left orientation, have united since 1994 in the Forum of the Third Sector, which has now become a key player in these issues and a partner of the government in the development of welfare and social policies. Here again, gaining institutional recognition comes at the price of a lower ability to mobilise for broader and more radical political campaigns.

In the Third Sector, however, there is great potential for social organisation and for new and more meaningful employment, as documented by much work carried out in particular by the association Lunaria. The book Lavori Scelti estimated that up to 200,000 jobs could be created by giving formal recognition to activities already carried out in civil society, often in the form of voluntary action.[2] In January 1998 new legislation was introduced regarding the legal status and fiscal incentives of 'non profit organisations of social utility' (ONLUS) and the field is now undergoing a rapid expansion. Current debates focus on the need for specific employment contracts in the social economy and on the potential for a basic income granted to young people involved in socially useful activities.

The dynamism of Third Sector organisations has much to do with the presence of a large number of volunteers, which represent a major force in Italian society. The IREF Report has calculated that in the field of social assistance and solidarity alone 13,000 groups, mainly with Catholic roots, are active in Italy with a million people regularly offering some of their time for voluntary action.[3] The forms of voluntary work are increasingly speeding into the fields of environment and cultural heritage, building new professional and training paths for young people.

---

1. Gian Paolo Barbetta, *Senza scopo di lucro. Il settore non profit in Italia*, Il Mulino, Bologna 1996.
2. Lunaria-Forum permanente del Terzo settore, *Lavori scelti*, Edizioni Gruppo Abele, Turin 1997.
3. IREF, *Sesto Rapporto sull'associazionismo sociale*, Rome, IREF 1998.

Alongside the search for alternative forms of production, great progress has been made in the fields of fair trade, ethical finance and awareness in consumption patterns. In Italy hundreds of fair trade shops can now be found offering Third World goods, from coffee and tea to textiles, traded in more equitable ways in co-operation with the international organisations of the field. A new Ethical Bank is opening in early 1999, established with funds provided by 8000 members of the founding co-operative. Consumption issues have seen the growth of boycott campaigns and educational activities all over the country. A new politics of lifestyle is taking hold in the country, catching up with the more advanced North European experiences.

A more direct political nature marks, on the other hand, the approximately one hundred Centri sociali *(Social Centres) which emerged in the early 1990s on the peripheries of several cities. Alongside political work in the area of the extreme left, they have built cultural and social activities, organising concerts and music productions, restaurants and courses, thereby offering employment and revenue to many of the people involved.*

A recent survey of the cultural productions of this area, Italia overground, *listed 63 magazines and reviews, 10 independent radios, 44 bookstores, 53 small publishers, 19 record and CD labels, 110 theatres and art groups, 96 audio-visual producersand 17 Internet sites.[4] In the area of Rome,* Lavori auto-organizzati *investigated the activities, forms of organisation and employment of 114 co-operatives, associations and small businesses with a total of about 1000 employees and as many volunteers.[5]*

Some specific efforts to link up the political experiences of the Third Sector, Centri sociali *and critical trade unionists have also taken place at the initiative of several local groups and of the independent left newspaper* Il Manifesto. *Over the last two*

---

4.   On the experience of *Centri sociali*, see Sandrone Dazieri, *Italia overground*, Castelvecchi, Rome 1996.
5.   Martino Mazzonis and Erika Lombardi, *Lavori autorganizzati*, Lunaria, Rome 1998.

years four large conventions of grassroots activists have been convened for sharing the efforts at understanding the social and political changes specific to different parts of the country, and for rebuilding a network of political analysis and action.

Social mobilisation, however, is not found on the left alone. Recent years have seen the growth of secessionist pressure from the *Lega Nord* (Northern League), the spread of racist actions and local protests against foreign immigrants, and the continuing presence of a strong extreme right of fascist origin. The *Lega Nord* has been able to increase its base among the popular classes in many regions of the North, and only since September 1997 has this growing consensus been challenged, with two mass demostrations organised - in Venice by a coalition of political forces, associations and *Centri social*, and in Milan by the trade unions.

In the context of this fragmentation of initiatives, the movement which has maintained the greatest continuity with its political roots of the 1980s is the peace movement. Although it has lost its mass mobilisation ability, it has proved its ability to understand the new nature of conflicts in the post-cold war world, and to intervene with non-violent initiatives and solidarity work in the areas of crisis close to Italy. Not just in the former Yugoslavia and Albania, but also in Israel and Palestine, where Italian peace activists have for a decade organised annual visits, demonstrations and solidarity projects prepared jointly with Israeli peace and women's groups and with Palestinian organisations.

Although the decisions regarding Italy's participation in recent peace-keeping and peace-enforcing missions in the Balkans have been hotly debated in the Italian movement, there is general consensus for rejecting NATO operations and supporting actions carried out under the United Nations which provide space for the non-military activities of NGOs and peace and solidarity groups.

On the domestic front a peace and solidarity culture is also spreading, with the continuing growth of conscientious objectors (more than 50,000 in 1997) and with the activities of hundreds of local authorities in peace education and international solidarity. Also a growing stream of youth participation is directed to the summer work camps all over the world, and new programmes are expanding in this context, such as the European voluntary service.

The peace movement also pays more attention to the political dimension of its actions, and has been involved in issues such as immigration and anti-racism, and Third Sector and international solidarity; it is thus overcoming the fundamental limitation of social movements: their single-issue nature, the concentration on a specific campaign with little co-ordination of related themes and no broader political objectives. The road followed for a long time by the peace movement, and in particular by the Peace Association, has been to build broader coalitions on specific campaigns, importing an effective Anglo-American model of mobilisation.

For a decade, the coalition of peace groups Venti di Pace (Winds of peace) has demanded cuts in the military budget, disarmament and conversion of military activities, and has put forward a package of amendments to the government budget which are supported by MPs of several political forces. In the last two years some proposals have been accepted in the Parliamentary vote on the budget.

In the last four years the organisations, mainly Catholic-based, active in the Campaign for Banning Landmines and the activity of Emergency, a group providing on-site support for civilian war victims, have succeeded in mobilising public opinion and obtaining a law which bans the production of and trade in mines.

In the early 1990s a broader coalition of associations had launched the Campaign Democrazia é partecipazione (Democracy means participation), asking individual candidates in the political elections to subscribe to some basic commitments on the issues of peace and solidarity, and then monitoring their voting behaviour in Parliament. While in recent years this initiative has been stopped, due also to the electoral reforms introduced, it has remained one of the most ambitious attempts to establish a link between social movements and institutional politics.

The initiative with the highest political and international profile has been the project of the People's Assembly of the United Nations, established by the *Tavola della Pace* (Peace Roundtable), roughly including 150 associations and groups and as many local authorities active on peace issues. In September 1995, on the 50th anniversary of the foundation of the UN, 120 representatives of the world's peoples - members of civil society organisations, rather than government nominees, as at the UN - were invited to Perugia to demand the reform and democratisation of the United Nations. The participants, guests of the local authorities involved, also visited hundreds of Italian cities and villages presenting to local audiences the peace and human rights problems of their countries. A Forum of international experts and a 15 mile March from Perugia to Assisi with 100,000 people completed the event.

Two years later, in October 1997, the second People's Assembly of the United Nations met again in Perugia focusing on the need 'for an economy with justice'. The appeal launching the People's Assembly and the new March from Perugia to Assisi denounced the world economy as: 'becoming increasingly unjust and unsustainable. It kills more people than bombs do. It sows the seeds of war and strife, exacerbates poverty, unemployment and social exclusion. The gap between the rich minority and the impoverished majority of humanity is becoming deeper and deeper'.

The programme, organised in co-operation with the UNDP and the UN centre in Italy, and with several international networks of NGOs and campaigns, included more than 500 events with 180 representatives of the world's peoples - mainly activists, policy makers, trade unionists, members of co-operatives and organisers on social and economic issues. The programme included visits to Italian cities, and participating with dozens of experts in 13 forums in different cities, dealing with specific topics, including: international economic institutions; workers' rights; debt; local development; the popular economy; the environment; women; child exploitation. In the second People's Assembly in Perugia grassroots experiences were shared among the participants and a set of demands to international institutions and national governments was agreed in a final document. The Peace March to Assisi was held on 12 October on a reduced scale because of the earthquake that had rocked Umbria in the weeks before the event.

A third People's Assembly of the United Nations is now planned for September 1999 on the theme of social movements as agents of change, with an effort to turn this event even more into an international venture, a meeting point for global civil society.

The extent of local involvement in these actions on world economic issues has been remarkable, showing the ability of social movements and associations to face the challenges of globalisation and to confront supranational organisations. In contrast, political forces and trade unions have proved unable to act beyond their traditional focus on national economic issues.

Has national policy paid any attention to these actions? In cases such as the debate on the reform of the UN and the Rome conference establishing an International Criminal Court in July 1998, the Italian government has responded to some extent to the requests from civil society and to the proposals of the first People's Assembly of the UN, although the actual outcome of the international negotiations has left much to be desired.

While it is impossible to assess the overall relevance of social movements in contemporary Italy, a strong dynamism is evident in civil society, in spite of the lack of mass movements of the kind we knew in the 1970s and early 1980s. A gap is widening between the perspectives and visions of the social movements and the practice of institutional politics, with the actions of the centre-left Ulivo government. This looks like a missed opportunity for a new politics in Italy and Europe, but confirms at the same time the continuing radical and original nature of some experiences of Italian social and political movements.

Further reading in this area: Giulio Marcon, *Italian Volunteers in Europe*, Lunaria, Rome 1996; A. Bonetti *et al.* *The Third Sector in Europe: Overview and Analysis, working paper of the NETS project*, Universita La Sapienza, Lunaria, Roma 1998; V. Mastrostefano, A. Messina and P. Naticchioni, *Review of present policies in Italy, working paper of the NETS project*, Universita La Sapienza, Lunaria, Roma 1998; E. Lombardi, A. Messina, O. Polimanti, *The forms of employment and work organisation in the Italian third sector, working paper*, Lunaria, Roma, 1998.

Political opposition in the Ivory Coast

Problems and perspectives

Richard Moncrieff

Richard Moncrieff analyses recent political events in the Ivory Coast.

At the beginning of 1990 the Ivory Coast, a country of 12 million people in West Africa, was thrown into chaos by a series of protests and strikes. The incidents started with a power cut in a university hall of residence in the capital Abidjan on 19 February, just before scheduled mid year exams (the whole academic year was later annulled). A small riot started and a handful of activists of the then clandestine opposition were arrested. Later the same week a group of students occupied the capital's cathedral and were also arrested. The next week protests grew, culminating in widespread rioting throughout the country on the 2 March. The direct grievance of the protesters was planned budget cuts, particularly in public sector salaries. However protests were not limited to the issue of budget cuts - the President was often a direct target of the crowd's anger and the lack of multiparty democracy in the country become another major grievance. Although in March the country became more peaceful, the real fear of the business and political élite was of a general strike. In the event the absence of independent unions and a ban on union meetings averted this, but sectoral strikes by teachers, the police and most damagingly by the transport workers along with demonstrations and occasional rioting continued throughout March and April. The persistence of protests, despite the government scrapping part of the budget cuts in mid April, finally forced the government to accept the re-legalisation of opposition parties on 5 May. Thirty years after opposition had been effectively banned at independence in 1960, the Ivory Coast entered a new political phase, with competitive presidential and parliamentary elections scheduled for later in the year.

These events were of particular importance due to the position of the then President Felix Houphouet-Boigny who, having survived in power for thirty years and being the president of a regionally important country, had become a key figure in the Paris centred constellation of power which still dominates the sub-region. Post colonial Africa has of course had its fair share of autocratic leaders and tyrants, but the former French colonies of West and Central Africa have followed a unique historical path. France has maintained particularly close institutional and personal ties with African leaders and has guaranteed the survival of regimes by regular military intervention. Having a more successful economy than most others up to the late 1980s, the Ivory Coast government has received particularly strong support from the French. As a result the Ivory Coast has been notably 'stable' with no civil war or coups. The other side of this stability has been the repression of dissent and the exclusion of the population from the political process. Furthermore the stability of the Ivorian state has not brought any meaningful development for the country's population. As elsewhere in Africa the introduction of multiparty elections has only succeeded to a limited extent in bringing democratic choice to the people. In this article I shall look at the reasons for this and I shall argue that the creation of a strong and principled opposition party or parties is one of the major and most urgent challenges facing this African country.

The underlying cause of the events of 1990 was the ruling élite's inability to cope with the debt crisis on the basis of an economy chronically dependent on the price of two commodities - cocoa and coffee. From the early days of independence the Ivorian élite had gambled heavily on agricultural export commodities, the high prices of the 1960s and 1970s encouraging them not to diversify the country's agricultural and industrial base. The relatively successful agricultural export sector was heavily taxed by means of a government purchasing body which bought all the raw produce at a price far below world market prices and sold it on to international trading companies. The ruling élites used the money to buy support around the country and attract new political activists into the single political party - the Democratic Party of the Ivory Coast (PDCI) - hence enabling it to buy off potential opposition while creating pockets of development. When world market prices for cocoa dropped by over half between January 1986 and July 1988 the PDCI no longer had the money to buy off criticism. The President, originally a farmers' union leader, refused to lower the price paid to farmers for the crops, thus effectively reversing the flow of resources from the government to the farmers and emptying the government's reserves.

As businesses started going bankrupt and jobs were lost, the President himself became a symbol of the country's growing inequality. In the mid-1970s he had ordered the construction of a huge catholic basilica in his native village of Yamoussoukro, a church which was to be the biggest in Africa. Alongside this a sumptuous presidential palace and an enormous conference centre were planned. All three were duly constructed at great cost but the village failed to become the new capital the President hoped it would. In a country lacking an adequate water supply, with a basic education system cracking at the seams and a chronic shortage of basic medical supplies, the buildings of Yamoussoukro stand today in eerie silence as an astonishing symbol of waste and vanity. When questioned about the financing of the basilica the President answered in March 1989 that the money came from his own pocket. When questioned later in October 1989, he replied, 'my account book is closed and placed at the foot of the Lord. Only God may know what I possess'. What we mortals do know is that he accumulated a personal fortune to be compared to Mobutu's and put most of it in Swiss bank accounts, having asked the press in 1983, 'what sensible man does not put some of his wealth in Switzerland?' Meanwhile his country was bankrupt and under the familiar guidance of the IMF's debt rescheduling and structural adjustment programmes. The subsequent wage cuts, job losses and losses of essential services were the reasons behind the waves of protest in 1990. What the events of 1990 showed is that when hardship reaches a certain point sustained resistance can bring real change. Opposition leaders still look at the legalisation of opposition parties as a major step in the right direction for their country. However just to be legalised doesn't mean you have a strong opposition up and running; major obstacles still stood in their way. To understand this one first needs to understand the remarkable strength of the ruling party and its leaders in the history of the Ivory Coast as an independent country.

Before 1990 - the Ivory Coast as a one party state

The survival of the PDCI and of President Houphouet-Boigny long after independence owed much to their role in fighting French colonialism and the respect this won them. Houphouet-Boigny first gained notoriety when as an MP in the French Parliament in 1946 he successfully proposed a law banning forced labour in the colonies. In the 1950s in the Ivory Coast the PDCI was harshly repressed by the colonial authorities that were fearful of the support it was getting from the Ivorian population. Most of the party's activists were arrested and Houphouet-Boigny's life was in danger more than once. This tactic on the part of the French failed to work and the PDCI continued to build its country-wide support. The colonial administration tried to counter its influence by creating and supporting a host of opposition parties. It is clear that at that time the role of opposition parties was to divide the Ivorian population and thereby to perpetuate French rule. This also failed.

By the time independence came in 1960 the PDCI had already created a *de facto* one party state. However with no credible rivals to campaign against on the ground, the PDCI became cut off from its popular base and was transformed into a vehicle for the personal ambitions of its leadership, which was more and more concentrated around the President. In 1958 Houphouet-Boigny was simultaneously president of the PDCI, an MP and a minister in Paris, Mayor of Abidjan and President of the Territorial Assembly. A series of purges of opponents and rivals in the early 1960s, the absorption of all union, student and political activity into the PDCI and a turn in policy towards supporting French interests ensured twenty years of almost unchallenged rule. The key element in Houphouet-Boigny's containment of dissent was a clever blend of heavy handed authoritarianism and symbolic reconciliation. He created a climate of fear in the country by regularly arresting and imprisoning opponents: then he released and publicly forgave them a couple of years into a life sentence. Clearly, observing the careers of other African leaders taught him that continual harsh repression would eventually backfire.

As with all single-party states the political system was based on a fictitious national unity. The entire population of the country were supposedly members of the party, and jobs and student grants depended on this membership. Of course within such a system the separation of powers was unimaginable - parliament, the judiciary and the administration were all absorbed by the party which itself was a vehicle for the ambitions of its leader. Some attempts were made to allow for political plurality in the early 1980s by allowing competition for party nominations for elections. However with no competition over programmes this experiment merely served to underline the limits of the one-party system. One-party elections remained a way of settling rivalries and promotions within the party and also served as an attempt to create a personality cult around the President through 100 per cent results at elections.

After 1990 - a difficult climate for opposition parties

The most important opposition party was until recently the Ivorian Popular Front (FPI), led by the historian Laurent Gbagbo. Other important parties exist - the Ivorian Workers Party (PTI) and the Ivorian Socialist Party (PSI) - alongside a plethora of smaller and largely insignificant ones. Laurent Gbagbo was the opposition's official candidate in the presidential elections of 1990 and achieved what most consider a respectable 18 per cent of the vote, given that it only had a few months as a legal party in which to organise its campaign. The FPI was formed by Gbagbo in 1982. It existed as a clandestine opposition for eight years and has now enjoyed eight years as a recognised opposition party. Throughout this time its struggle to become a credible opposition has been conditioned by several factors: the continued strength of the PDCI establishment, even after the death of President Houphouet-Boigny in December 1993, continual disputes over electoral procedures which have often spilt over into clashes with the police; the tensions between ideological opposition on the one hand and regional and sectional opposition on the other; and the problem of alliances with other opposition parties.

The PDCI élite has retained its control over the Ivorian police, military and administrative structures and has used this to suppress opposition activity. The much boasted freedom of the press (newspapers close to the opposition parties are freely available) has been tempered by the government's willingness to imprison over-critical journalists. A law dating from 1959 has made it illegal to 'Throw discredit on political institutions or their functioning'. More than fifteen journalists were sent to prison between December 1993 and January 1996. The appalling conditions and cholera epidemics of Ivorian prisons ensure that this is a strong deterrent. According to *Le Monde* one journalist who had the temerity to criticise the interior minister was beaten by the police in the minister's office with the minister looking on. Some newspapers have been temporarily banned, including the influential *Jeune Afrique*. Although opposition candidates are allowed some air time at elections, the state run television is clearly pro-government, the long evening news acting as a eulogy to the latest government public works programme.

> 'As with all single-party states the political system was based on a fictitious national unity'

Opposition leaders, as well as other prominent figures such as the president of the Ivorian Human Rights League, claim that both the two legislative elections and the two presidential elections held since the legalisation of opposition parties have been marked by fraud and mismanagement. One of the opposition's major campaign points is the setting up of a truly independent electoral commission. Voting papers, it is claimed, are regularly simply bought by local PDCI officials. Disputes often break out as members of the opposition are prevented from observing vote counting. Moreover the campaigns are spoilt by the difficulties which the opposition encounter in getting permission to hold meetings. Finally there are bitter disputes over the validity of electoral lists. However the opposition parties themselves are not free from blame in terms of hindering free and fair elections. In 1995, after disputes concerning the nationality criteria of candidates, they declared an 'active boycott' which in many cases took the form of disrupting the voting procedure and preventing others voting. Detailed discussion of policy or of the country's problems was lost in dispute over electoral procedure, which ultimately played into the hands of the ruling party and was a loss for the Ivory Coast's young democracy.

One of the main problems for opposition parties is reaching a critical mass of support in order to be seen as a potential winner. In a country so dominated by the party in power, voting, financial and activist support show a strong tendency to go to the candidates who are perceived as having the best chance of winning. This is further reinforced by a first-past-the-post constituency voting system which ensures that the party with the largest percentage of the vote gets an even larger percentage of parliamentary seats. Remaining in opposition when favours and resources are distributed between those close to the government can be a frustrating experience. The material means and labour time needed to organise a party and gather the information needed to build a coherent alternative programme are simply not available. New parties generally start out by offering principled or ideological opposition, presenting a political programme of government argued from basic principles and designed to attract nation-wide support. However they are often forced to concentrate their resources in one region, and run the risk of representing the grievances of one ethnic group or else becoming isolated in one profession, notably the teaching profession, the source of most opposition activity in the Ivory Coast.

The 1995 elections showed that this situation can be disastrous for the opposition. Unable to create a strong nation-wide support they played on the grievances of minority ethnic groups (exacerbated by very uneven regional development). This is an unfortunate development in Ivorian politics as even among the PDCI élite there is little evidence of one ethnic group being dominant. Since independence the 'national unity' policy of the one party state, despite its drawbacks, did play down ethnic divisions. For the 1995 elections the PDCI responded by rewriting the electoral code to exclude foreigners from voting and from candidacy - essentially an attempt to grab the 'race card' for themselves. In the furore which followed, the two strongest opposition candidates - Laurent Gbagbo and Alassane Ouattara - refused to stand. It is still a disputed point whether or not Ouattara was effectively barred by the new law due to his disputed parentage. (It is claimed that his parents come from Burkina-Faso, although he maintains that he is Ivorian). Another opposition leader - Francis Wodié - decided to stand, signalling the break-up of the opposition alliance. Lacking a support base, Wodié obtained only 3.5 per cent of the vote. The abstention rate was high, which the opposition claimed as a victory for their 'active boycott'. In several areas voting was totally disrupted by clashes between rival party supporters and with the police. Although this took some legitimacy away from the victory of Henri Konan Bedié (the PDCI candidate and effective heir of Houphuoet-Boigny), the opposition were probably more damaged by their failure to contest the election. The legislative elections which followed confirmed this as the PDCI won 147 out of 175 seats with the opposition putting up competing candidates in 71 constituencies. Five years after opposition parties had been legalised, the PDCI elite looked to be in a stronger position than ever.

The emergence of Allassane Ouattara's new party - the RDR - in 1994 brought a new kind of party into Ivorian Politics. While the FPI had always tried to present itself as a centre-left opposition to the centre-right PDCI, the RDR is a party of technocrats which has emerged from the PDCI itself. Ouattara, a former deputy head at the IMF and Ivorian finance minister, enjoys a network of powerful supporters both at home and abroad unrivalled by any other opposition leader. He offers the credibility that the opposition so desperately needs, but fails to offer the sort of discussion over fundamental principles which has traditionally been the lifeblood of politics.

Different kinds of opposition

Parallels with the Ivorian case of partial democratisation can be found throughout Africa. I would like to argue that the Ivorian case also reveals some important points concerning the role and importance of opposition parties in African states, almost all of which have until recently endured several decades of one-party rule. Firstly, opposition is part of the very principle of democracy, offering the people a choice of who they wish to be governed by. Secondly, in countries plagued by the financial corruption of the ruling élite, an opposition is clearly needed, along with an independent press, to provide a check on government activities and to expose corruption publicly. For this they must have adequate resources to gather information independently from government sources. Thirdly, opposition parties must provide a real chance of a change of government. Under the PDCI the lines between the business, administrative and political élites blurred to the point of disappearing. In such a situation only a change of government can begin to establish some sort of separation of powers. Even if the government does not actually change, the very possibility of change can act as a check on those in power.

These functions of an opposition can feasibly be performed in the Ivory Coast by Ouattara's RDR. However a political opposition is needed in order to play other roles and here I fear that the RDR may not be so suited. Firstly, an opposition should involve the whole population of a country in debate over how that country is run and should be run. We have already seen that the Ivory Coast's traditional opposition parties are under-resourced to perform this task. The FPI is currently undertaking a country-wide tour of meetings in an attempt to correct this. It is questionable whether it has the money to sustain it. On the other hand, the RDR may have the resources to do so. However it is essentially a party already within the Ivorian political elite and made up of former PDCI technocrats and officials. It remains to be seen to what extent they engage with the concerns of the mass of the population in the run-up to the elections of 2000.

Secondly, an opposition is needed in order to present a coherent set of alternative ideas concerning the government of the country. The principles a party supports need to be explicitly stated, otherwise voters will quickly become disillusioned with the democratic process, suspecting that it consists of replacing one set of crooks with another. Of course a party elected on a principled platform can quickly succumb to the temptations and difficulties of being in power, but nevertheless the whole possibility of meaningful democratic debate depends ultimately on arguing from basic principles such as freedom and equality, pragmatism and idealism. To their credit the FPI has always tried to do this, producing books, newspapers and even cassettes explaining its

'An opposition must have adequate resources to gather information independently from government sources'

position. Equally, a principled ideological stance can help avoid the ethnicisation of politics by providing a real debate on the political issues which cut across ethnic boundaries. Unfortunately, with the dominance of the PDCI élite, Ivorian politics in the years leading up to Houphouet-Boigny's death in December 1993 was dominated by the question of leadership succession from within the PDCI. In the event, Houphouet-Boigny's designation of Bedié as the leader of Parliament and therefore constitutional successor in the event of his death was a more decisive event in terms of future leadership of the country than the campaign around the presidential elections two years later. This effectively amounted to the traditional élites choosing their own successor with no reference to the country's population.

Foreign actors in African politics, and particularly aid donors, have recently turned their attention to supporting 'civil society' in an apparent attempt to allow room for expression and activity at a distance from the traditional political élites. The problem with this is that in the desperate rush to appear ever more liberal and business-friendly it becomes easy to confuse 'civil society' with commercial interests, which of course are already very close to and well supported by the political élites. As Marina Ottaway has pointed out, civil society is either too close to government or too fragmented to ensure that a government behaves responsibly: this can only be done by a strong opposition.[1] Unfortunately but unsurprisingly, foreign aid and backing has always been used to support incumbent regimes, all in the name of 'stability'. (In 1990 the PDCI accused the FPI of most unfairly receiving a small amount of support from the French Socialist Party. The 'accusations' were largely true but were evidently absurd coming from a party hugely supported by the French for three decades.)

Of course it is bitterly ironic that opposition parties emerged in a legal way in Africa just as the very idea of ideological politics was being actively destroyed in Europe. However the concept and reality of political opposition must now be taken seriously and allowed political space to develop in the Ivory Coast and elsewhere in Africa. As Laurent Gbagbo has said: 'democracy is an act of humility. It is taking into account the relativity of individual intelligence and of doctrines ... to be a democrat is to recognise that one does not have a monopoly over truth, wisdom or the love of one's country.'[2] It has been argued here that the legacy of forty years of autocratic presidential rule in the Ivory Coast, wherein political conflict and change occurred between a leader and a successor, not between a leader and an opponent, is ill-suited to a situation where the leader commands a large country with potentially rich resources. Although at certain times national unity rightly takes priority (as during the decolonisation period), those who still argue that ideological opposition is a distraction from the real job of national social and economic development are ignoring the record of waste and corruption under Africa's single party states.

---

1. Marina Ottoway, 'African Democratisation and the Leninist Option', in *Journal of Modern African Studies* 35, 1. 1997.
2. Laurent Gbagbo, *Cote d'Ivoire: Pour une alternative démocratique*, Harmattan, Paris 1983, p153.

Technology, economics and the future

Sean Gray

Diane Coyle, *The Weightless World*, Capstone Press

Hardly a week passes without another book about globalisation. Most consist of little more than a dazzled gape at the wonders of modern technology and a claim that we must abandon this or that part of our belief system as a result. Occasionally there are more thoughtful and reflective interventions. *Soundings* has published several of these.[1] Diane Coyle's *The Weightless World* is another.

Diane Coyle's contribution to the globalisation debate is to say that the real development is not globalisation but weightlessness. In this way she counters the arguments of those, like Hirst and Thompson, who point out that, by many measures, the world economy at the end of the nineteenth century was as global as at the end of the twentieth. She argues that, because of the phenomenon of weightlessness, international forces have been given a greater leverage - not because powerful groups such as corporations or governments are more international, but because the obstacles to international interaction are diminished. While globalisation is a slogan attached to a contested description of locality, weightlessness has the merit of offering an account of why change might happen. It opens the way to analysis and discussion.

At this point we need to examine the concept of weightlessness more closely.

---

1. See, for example, D. Massey, 'Problems with Globalisation', *Soundings* 7; P. Hirst and G. Thompson, 'Globalisation: Ten frequently asked questions and some surprising answers', *Soundings* 4 ; D. Goldblatt, D. Held, A. McGrew, J. Perraton, 'Economic Globalisation and the nation state; the transformation of political power' *Soundings* 7.

Does the idea really get us any further than globalisation? At one level weightlessness is, as its name suggests, a negative concept. It means that technology has changed so that we can now meet the same wants and needs with lighter products. The book illustrates this with the fact that there is more computing power in a contemporary speaking birthday card than existed in the whole world in 1950. We have tended traditionally to think of weight as good measure of economic value: two tonnes of steel are twice as good as one; and even two tonnes of machinery are roughly worth twice as much as one tonne. With electronic products this is clearly no longer the case. Weight is not what matters. In particular, the development of information technology has meant that economic resources can be deployed cleverly rather than massively. To Diane Coyle this dramatic change in what one might think of as an economic power-to-weight ratio offers a clue to fundamental changes in our conceptions of space and time. And, as a way of looking at the economic and political impact of technological change, the concept of weightlessness has advantages over the concept of globalisation. It is more fundamental; it looks at what the technology does rather than at what its consequences are assumed to be; and it comes unladen with the political agenda which globalisation has acquired. However, there are also some problems with the way in which the term is used, which I will outline later.

This review will look at where the concept of weightlessness takes Diane Coyle, and also at where else it might take us. Coyle uses her concept to look at the prospects for democratic control of capitalist economies, the role of financial markets, the future of work, urbanisation and the development of inequality. This is a useful agenda, even if the conclusions she reaches are not ones with which I would always agree. My aim is to engage with some of the items on this agenda, and also to look at some new areas where the concept of weightlessness might lead to interesting developments.

Weightless work

Diane Coyle sees weightlessness as the kind of new technology which creates jobs rather than destroys them. She is optimistic about the prospects for jobs. She sees the growing need for caring, and the technical advances which come from weightlessness, as generating millions of jobs. Here her conclusions might be right, but her arguments are slightly awry. Weightlessness is not the cause of the increasing need for caring work. There will no doubt be an increasing need for work in this area, if, as at present appears to be the case, people - in rich countries at least - get older faster than they get fitter. That in itself, however, has nothing to do with weightlessness. Equally, the technical changes associated with weightlessness - those which reduce the weight of traditionally heavy activities such as manufacturing - do not, simply because they are themselves weightless, act as a stimulus to activity in these fields of work, which have always been weightless. Any technical progress, whether weighty or not, might create the space in which resources can be released for caring; and it might or might not destroy jobs in traditional industries. The fact that caring is weightless is irrelevant.

Another misleading elision is evident in the book's faith in finance. Finance is seen as a harbinger of the weightless world. However, many people work in a weightless way. The fact that operators in finance do so, and indeed have effectively done so ever since the invention of credit, does not mean, as the book implies, that the future, and, by implication, the truth, lies with banking, or that financiers understand the world any better than anyone else. One might as easily point to the writers of fairy stories, the designers of computer games, or teachers of economics, as similar harbingers of the weightless world. All pursue weightless economic activities. But the future does not lie with activities which have always been weightless. The big changes will come with those activities which have *become* weightless. If becoming weightless leads to greater efficiency - as the book reasonably assumes - it can then release resources, and weightless activities like caring can take greater prominence.

Weightlessness and the threat to democracy

The popular concept of globalisation implies a belief that production has become freer to move - at the passing of a whim, the enhancement of an environmental standard, or the pressing of a pay claim. The threat which internationally mobile capital is seen to present to democracy and social progress is therefore thought to be enhanced by the greater mobility which weightlessness brings. In fact, globalisation in general, and the technological phenomena which have given it a further twist, are little more than excuses for reiterating long held and traditional arguments. Debates about the feasibility of democratic economics in capitalist society are merely recast into a new context. The substantive issues have changed relatively little.

In this area the book is closer to orthodox economics, basing its pessimism on the antique nostrums of conventional economic theory rather than any new analysis. It offers no convincing evidence that the forms of new technology driving the weightless world have had any effects which might lead to the modification of the traditional arguments. It spares us the 'gee-whiz billions of dollars zipping across the exchanges every nano-second' kind of argument. But its belief in the inevitability of international capital markets' restricting governments' freedom of manoeuvre is actually based largely on wish fulfilment and some selective historical examples. Coyle cites, as do many, the case of the Mitterrand government in the early 1980s, as illustrating the inevitability of the failure of democratic governments to control their economies. The example is inevitably controversial, but the main point it makes is that Mitterrand was the victim of *political* interventions from aboard. International capital markets were to a large extent the channel through which France's economic ambitions were brought down by German, British and US politicians. That may teach us important political lessons, but not that there was anything intrinsically or technically wrong with Mitterrand's policy. In fact the freeing of international capital markets has probably made it easier for governments to raise funds and pursue independent economic policies. Increasingly, economic theory and theories of globalisation play an ideological role in restraining governments from exercising these freedoms, by convincing them that they cannot be exercised.

At times Coyle herself comes close to conceding that governments might have the power to defy the dictates of international capital markets, but she argues that it is just as well that they do not believe that they have such a power. She welcomes the restraints placed on governments by international markets. She sees the markets as preventing governments from doing what they might otherwise be tempted to do to try to maintain full employment or public services. She describes the international capital markets as, 'the only voice raised against excessive future taxes that will have to be raised to service current government borrowing'. But the voice being raised here is not technical – it is the ideological voice of economic orthodoxy.

But not all economists agree that weightlessness restrains governmental plans for economic expansion. One of Diane Coyle's heroes, Allan Greenspan of the US Federal Reserve Board, has suggested that weightlessness will enhance governments' ability to foster economic expansion, because there will be fewer physical constraints. He believes that weightlessness means that the economy can grow faster. So one of the key figures in world finance actually sees weightlessness as leading to less need for vigilance to restrain expansionist economic policies.

Inequality

Technically driven globalisation is also held responsible for the maintenance of inequality and poverty in industrial countries. Because industries can migrate to low-cost countries, many analysts and commentators believe that globalisation has caused pay differentials between skilled and unskilled labour to deteriorate. They are wrong. In the first place, the deterioration in pay distribution is very much a UK and US phenomenon. Therefore it cannot be seen as the result of general forces which would affect all countries. Secondly, it is far from clear that low paid employment in rich countries is the sector which is most in competition with labour in poor countries. If one takes, for example, the Indian IT industry, the workers are highly skilled and highly paid by Indian standards. They are competing with highly skilled workers in industrial countries who tend also to be paid well by local standards. Indeed, a large fraction of low paid jobs in rich countries are in service industries, which are not in competition with output from poor countries. Serving hamburgers remains a local activity. Those items which have become more mobile as a result of weightlessness tend on the whole to be skill intensive, which means that any downward pressure on wages should be felt more by those on high wages in industrial countries. Thus, if it has any effect in this area at all, weightlessness which enables production at a distance could, it seems, compress income distributions rather than expand them.

The book also uses the superstar-economy theories of Danny Quah to explore the link between weightlessness and inequality. [2] This theory argues that, as communication becomes easier, then those endowed with special talents will increasingly acquire more of the world's wealth, because people will be less inclined to settle for second best. It should be acknowledged that at one point Coyle concedes that the theory could equally go the other way - greater communication could lead to a greater variety of tastes and more superstars. But in either case, the argument reflects an economist's naive belief that income is a reflection of talent or skill, rather than of command over resources.

---

2. D. Quah, 'The invisible hand and the weightless economy', London School of Economics Centre for Economic Performance Occasional Paper no 12, May 1996.

Non-market production

Given her radicalism about the future of work, Diane Coyle is relatively timid about the impact that weightlessness might have on economic organisation. She sees the traders on today's financial markets as the leaders in a trend which illustrates the way the weightless economy will work. This may be true, but it is equally arguable that the market system itself may become obsolete. This is because many of the outputs of weightless production are very hard to market. They are what economists refer to as public goods. Once they have been produced, anyone can use them. In technical economist's parlance, they will be non-rivalrous, and could be non-excludable. An example of a non-rivalrous product is broadcasting, where one person's listening or watching does not prevent another person's doing so. Broadcasting was traditionally seen as non-excludable as well - it is difficult to prevent someone receiving a broadcast. Much research is being undertaken aiming at enabling broadcasters to exclude viewers so that they can charge them, but the bulk of broadcasting - whether public service or commercial - relies on charging advertisers for access to the non-exclusive broadcasts, rather than directly charging listeners or viewers. Similarly, charging over the Internet is also proving challenging, both to the commercial organisations which would like to profit from it, and to the liberal ethos which pervades much of its use. By contrast, low technology weightless products such as personal services are more easily turned into commodities. A weightless capitalist economy may therefore continue the commodification of personal services. It may also seek to develop new public sector institutions to control the production of high technology weightless products. This means we could see care privatised and weightless production nationalised. Thus weightlessness may have very different effects from those expected, because of the status of many weightless products as public goods.

Economic theory, even of the most orthodox kind, suggests that public goods provide a case for state intervention. We could therefore be on the threshold of an ideological revival of state productive activity. In the first half of the twentieth century the socialist arguments for public ownership, which were based on the ending of exploitation, were reinforced by arguments for efficiency. It was widely believed that, with the emergence of large-scale production, the pursuit of technical efficiency led to inefficient concentrations of economic power, and the development of cartels, etc. Economic theory suggested that one way of dealing with this was to have state companies which could ensure the benefits of large-scale production without such attendant dangers. Thirty years of sustained counter-attack has now destroyed the efficiency argument as far as traditional production is concerned - although in practice most capitalist countries retain a very large state productive sector. But, at the end of the century, weightlessness is bringing a new generation of productive activities which are vital to the development of capitalism, but which may not be effectively delivered by private capital. Just as the state had to maintain infrastructure such as railways or telephones in the past, so it may have to support weightless communications systems such as the Internet if traditional private capital fails.

Weightlessness could be bringing us closer to the world of Wells and Orwell than anyone in recent years has imagined. For capitalism to operate in a world of weightlessness it must find some way of creating commodities. At present the effort is focused on making electronic products excludable. An alternative is to use the state to produce non-excludable products. Diane Coyle offers another route - a set of excludable weightless products - care. Care commodities are not high tech. They are the fruits of technological advances only because they leave people with the longevity to need, and sufficient income to afford, higher standards of care. It is not clear whether care commodities can save capitalism, but the question provides an interesting focus.

Is the weightless world the future we have been expecting?

We have arrived in some ways at the world which was described by the pessimistic analysts of the 1950s in terms of the problem of plenty. They asked what would people do when technology had eliminated hunger and disease. Obviously that has not happened even in the wealthiest nations, let alone in most countries. But there has certainly been a reduction in the material causes of deprivation in rich industrial countries. This has not led, as the question implied, to the obsolescence of labour. There has been a massive growth in employment in personal services. Some has been through their commodification, transferring production from non-market to market sectors, but much of it has been in the kind of services which people have in the past done without. Coyle's response to that question now is that the same thing will continue. People will work at personal services. That seems to me to be her key theoretical insight -

that people's needs for personal services are very large. The evolution of capitalism will be determined by the way in which it can turn such personal services into commodities.

Diane Coyle may, one suspects, still have short-circuited some of the mystifications which lie ahead in this process, but she is pointing in a direction which has distinguished forebears. In this, as in many other areas, she has looked through superficial relations to find some more enduring and reliable features of society. It is that search which we all need to continue.

A liberal humanist in Hong Kong

Aasiya Lodhi

Chris Patten, *East and West*, Macmillan, £22.50

The image of Chris Patten weeping in the monsoon rain on that final day of colonial rule in Hong Kong is one which will be remembered for the rather un-English show of emotion. The Last Governor had undoubtedly gone through one of the most unique experiences in the half-century of British decolonisation - not preparing the way for independence but handing over to one of the world's most ancient empires. This experience 'shaped and marked' him, he says, more than any other in his political life. If that was not enough to guarantee an eager, expectant readership for the story of those five years, then Rupert Murdoch's highly publicised rejection of the manuscript - and the resignation of his publishing director - certainly was. The book, it was rumoured, was so virulent an attack on the Chinese government that Murdoch had decided to drop it for fear of jeopardising his commercial interests in China.

Unfortunately *East and West* is neither the scathing attack on China and the Foreign Office which most readers hoped for, nor a riveting account of Patten's daily battles as governor. Some of this weakness lies in its structure - the book is part memoir, part political manifesto and part economic theory. But the most surprising and disappointing element is that Patten has been very circumspect about naming his opponents and critics. There are numerous stinging references to Foreign Office mandarins, whom Patten divides into two groups - the OCH (Old China Hands)and the OFOCs (Old Friends of China); but not even the venerable Sinologue Sir Percy Cradock, whose animosity towards Patten was well known, gets a mention. Similarly, the Beijing leadership are named in passing, but discreetly erased from any specific criticisms of China's behaviour in the run-up to 1997. This may well be because Patten is now hoping to revive his political career, and indeed parts of the book read as an extended C.V. But the patent airbrushing of key players - well-known to have been involved in rows with the governor - has created a book of marginal interest for those readers anxiously awaiting a detailed account of Patten's side of the story.

What is left is an eloquent if somewhat unoriginal thesis on 'Asian values' and the links between political freedom and economic success. Patten asserts that there is no Asian value system which can account for the huge success of the tiger economies; an emphasis on the family, a privileging of community before self, and a rejection of pluralist forms of political representation are not the ingredients of a magic formula which lay behind the Asian economic 'miracle'. East is the same as West in this respect - the free market is the base for political liberty but one cannot exist indefinitely without the other. For too long the 'invented concept of Asian values' has been used as 'an excuse for Westerners to close their eyes to abuses of human rights in Asia'. Now that the miracle is over - a clear sign for Patten that economic and political liberalism go hand in hand - he is even keener to stress that without democratic systems in place, the idea of the (21st) Pacific century is mere chimera. Indonesia and, more recently, Malaysia are prime examples. The economic and political turmoil that swept Indonesia in 1997 and ended in Suharto's resignation was indicative of the fact that crony capitalism and corruption - the hallmarks of the undemocratic state - ultimately lead to chaos. There is glowing praise for the liberal-minded Malaysian (now ex-) Finance Minister Anwar Ibrahim, battling against the protectionist attitudes of Dr Mahathir.

However, Patten is most authoritative when talking about Hong Kong - for him it is the perfect model of his absolute belief in economic liberalism. It is a city which has transformed itself into one of the most dynamic and prosperous countries in the region; where its residents are free from fear of a 'midnight knock at the door', certain they will be able to afford to look after their elderly relatives, confident they will be able to give their children a good education. This was achieved, in Patten's view, under the auspices of a hands-off approach by Britain, but he is the first to admit that the attitude towards democracy advanced by many of his predecessors was hardly praiseworthy. What Hong Kong needs now is greater freedom, not less, and one of Patten's greatest regrets is that the British government did not do enough to safeguard and facilitate this. Hong Kong 'deserved better of Britain' he says in one of the more poignant moments in the book, 'and I fear the people we left behind know it.' Amongst these people would surely be leading pro-democracy activists such as Martin Lee and Emily Lau, whom Patten thoroughly praises, hoping they will continue to fight to secure a lasting form of democracy in Hong Kong.

Whilst Patten's promotion of political as well as economic freedom is certainly laudable, this is hardly a groundbreaking analysis. Regrettably the Hong Kong government's interventionist moves in the economy occurred too recently to be included in the book. What would Patten make of this? Somehow you get the feeling that it would be subsumed, like many other glaring anomalies, into the over-arching cause of glorifying liberalism. This is in fact exactly what happens when the myriad problems of many other East Asian countries are tackled. Singapore's iron grip on political and civil liberties is ferociously attacked (a city-state where critics of the government are 'pursued by defamation suits through the courts'), but what of the fact that it has weathered the economic crisis better than most of its neighbours? There is surprisingly little about South Korea, and virtually no mention of Japan. Neither is there any recognition of other key factors in the Asian economic boom, such as the accessibility of cheap labour. The unswerving message is that 'good honest governance' is the answer to economic woes, and it is one which is hammered out at frequent intervals throughout the book - most fervently in the context of China.

There is also much talk of 'decency', Patten's favourite word. It is 'decent' politics which he hopes is his legacy to Hong Kong and will also one day become part of the Chinese political lexicon. Confucius, 'the victim of even more distortion and reinterpretation than Jesus of Nazareth', was the perfect embodiment of this; proof that the liberal tradition has Asian roots and that Asian culture is not inextricably linked to 'order, hierarchy, self-discipline and obedience'. Quoting rather selectively from the Analects, Patten maps out a liberal humanist paradigm with Confucian foundations in which he locates himself, the vocal defender of democracy.

Patten says he never really had to delve into the reasons why he was a democrat until he went to Hong Kong, having fallen into politics after finishing university almost by accident. Only when he took the job of Governor did he feel 'radicalized' in any way; the fervour which he never experienced in his youth stole upon him in middle age, finally turning him into a conviction politician. 'Hong Kong obliged me to think hard about the nature and causes of economic success, and the relationship between that success and politics', he says in the chapter entitled 'Back to the Future'. Whilst most of what Patten has thought long and hard about is fairly quotidian, his is a passionate and committed voice. And it's one which certainly won't remain unheard in the British political arena in the near future.

Eurocentrism through the backdoor

Nadje S. Al-Ali

Bobby Sayyid, *A Fundamental Fear: Eurocentrism and the Emergence of Islamism,* Zed Books

The bombings of the American embassies in Dar El Salam and Nairobi only confirmed what the British public 'knew' all along: Islamic fundamentalists - often simply thought of as 'Muslims' - are responsible for the bloodshed of innocent civilians. Subsequently, Britain, like many other European countries, and North America, experienced yet another series of racist outbursts equating terrorism with Islam. In light of these ongoing demonisations of Muslims and Islam, it is imperative to find forceful and creative arguments and practices to counter this increasingly widespread form of bigotry.

It is with this need in mind that I read Bobby Sayyid's recently published book. And it certainly is not another fear-mongering sensationalist outburst about bloodthirsty Muslims. Quite the contrary. It is one of the most comprehensive attempts by a British scholar to counter negative and paranoid portrayals of Islamism. Sayyid's project is to expose orientalism with respect to analyses of Islamism and to 'de-centre the West'.

So far, so fair. The trouble is that Sayyid builds up Islamism as the only viable alternative to western imperialism. This is factually wrong. And it is politically dangerous - for people living in far less safe and comfortable circumstances than Sayyid. It sells out the many women and men in 'Muslim societies' who are not only sturdy anti-imperialists but also secular.

When I discussed Sayyid's argument with feminists and human rights activists in Egypt, a country with growing Islamist movements, the outrage was coupled with a sense of *deja vu*. Bobby Sayyid is a sociology lecturer and the director of the Centre for the Study of Globalisation, Eurocentrism and Marginality at Manchester University. His book drops into the midst of the political battles of the local, lived realities of these activists, wearing the dustjacket of a western publishing house. So here was another western scholar giving himself the right to decide what would classify as 'authentic' and what would be a 'western import'. To them it looked just like one more front on which they had to struggle.

Sayyid positions himself clearly outside and critical of orientalist accounts that explain the 'Muslim world' exclusively in terms of Islam, its majority religion - that is characterised as 'essentialism'. What happens next though is that he himself adopts the essentialism - although one could be forgiven for missing this because he hides it in dense postmodernist code. Islam, he says, is a 'master signifier'. And so it acquires, in his hands, an unchanging and singular essence. All sense of diversity, of historical development, goes out of the window.

And this is specially paradoxical because Sayyid says in the same breath that 'there cannot be a universal definition of religion, not only because its constituent elements and relationships are historically specific, but because the definition is itself the historical product of discursive processes' (p15). This passage occurs in that moment in the book where he takes issue with Gita Sahgal and Nira Yuval-Davis for the way they use 'fundamentalism' as an analytical category in their book on women and religious fundamentalism in Britain.[1] For Sayyid they are two more in a line of 'western feminists' who see the world through a narrow lens of self-righteousness. To anyone familiar with these authors the attack is bewildering and distressing. These are both members of a London-based group of activists and writers called Women Against Fundamentalism (WAF). WAF is a group of feminists of highly varied cultural, national and religious background, well known for their effective campaigns against all forms of politico-religious extremism, and also their strong stand against racism, essentialism and eurocentrism. WAF have made clear from the

1. Gita Sahgal and Nira Yuval-Davis, 'Introduction: Fundamentalism, Multiculturalism and Women in Britain', in G. Saghal and N. Yuval-Davis (eds) *Refusing Holy Orders: Women and Fundementalism in Britain*, Virago, London, 1992.

start that they are not primarily critical of Islamic fundamentalism, but have mobilised against the oppression of women in the sexual and family politics of all forms of authoritarian patriarchal religious movements, not excluding Hinduism, Judaism and both Protestant and Catholic Christianity. It takes a good deal of inventiveness to be able, as Sayyid does, to misrepresent them so thoroughly as to be able to write them off as modernist, ethnocentrist and endorsing 'the homogeneity of the female subject' (p10).

Sayyid takes issue with the use of the word 'fundamentalist' by WAF and others as a western misrepresentation of current Islamist movements. WAF for their part argue that there are similarities and connections between political religious conservative movements in these various religions, and the way they operate in both western and non-western, Islamo-phobic and Islamist societies, that justify its use. Certainly, the term carries a heavy load, as the western media muddy the water by eliding Islam and fundamentalism. But when WAF uses the term 'fundamentalism' it is always made clear that it is intended in the plural, and not only Islamic fundamentalism is in question.

Sayyid ignores the different origins of Islamist movements, their varied ideologies, strategies, organisational forms and political and economic contexts. A sketchy mention at the very end of the book, where he acknowledges that 'there are many variations in Islamism as there are Islamist movements', is clearly an afterthought. In the body of his argument, Islamism is one thing and one thing only, and its emergence has one source.

And that source is the thrust to de-centre the West. It is a mono-causal explanation, featuring purely and simply resistance to eurocentrism (p155). Sayyid overlooks all the varied and specific social, economic and political circumstances that have contributed to the emergence of Islamism country by country. A complex phenomenon is reduced to singularity.

In representing the contemporary emergence of Islamism as nothing more than a move to 'de-centre the West', Sayyid gives overwhelming importance to 'the West' in the thinking of other regions. Islamist political actors are portrayed as merely motivated by the impetus of 'not being western' rather than acting on and reacting to other local factors such as economic and social malaise within specific countries, oppressive regimes and lack of political participation, or failures of secular ideologies, such as liberalism or socialism. The list of possible causes is long, but Sayyid dismisses other possible arguments as not adequately explaining why the challenge to the existing order has repeatedly and consistently taken the form of Islamic revivalism (p5). But this is an example of what Sami Zubaida calls reading history backwards; it ignores or dismisses 'secular and secularising forces, institutions and practices in the modern history of the Middle East and the lengthy episodes in which nationalist, liberal and leftist politics dominated'. [2]

There is one instance in his book where Sayyid does look in depth at an actual historical moment in a given local context: the secularising forces and programmes in Turkey after the abolition of the caliphate under Mustapha Kemal Ataturk in 1924. Modernisation, secularisation, nationalism and westernisation merged into a discourse and practice known as 'Kemalism'. Sayyid characterises Kemalism by the belief that Turkey had to emulate European culture, practices and values in order to achieve progress and 'become modern'. Islam was seen by Ataturk as a hindrance on the path to modernity.

This is a reasoned and vivid account. But why does Sayyid choose Kemalism as though it were the only secular paradigm in the Muslim world? It was, in fact, an exception, an anomaly, not the rule. Unlike any other secular model in the Middle East and the Muslim world, it was inspired by and based on the French concept of *laicisme*. One could draw on other Arab postcolonial projects, such as socialism and Arab nationalism, where the disassociation from Islam has never been as extreme as in Kemalism. What about Nasserism, Marxism, Ba'athism and the various forms of liberalism that, while not religious, have strongly countered western hegemony and imperialism? By neglecting these other and varied secular trends, Sayyid betrays those secular intellectuals and political activists in Muslim societies who have devoted their lives to the struggle against western hegemony.

In his discussion of Kemalism, Sayyid presupposes first that there is only one definition of Islam among Christians and it is orientalist; and second, that there is only one model of secularism within Christianity. In both of these things he is mistaken. He writes that 'the "Christian" (orientalist) definition of Islam removed it from the public-political domain' and that 'this notion of religion was modelled using the specific characteristics of Christianity as an exemplar' (p64). But there was no natural and inherent link between Christianity and secularism understood as the separation of religion and the state. This is to

---

2. Sami Zubaida, *Islam, the People and the State: Political Ideas and Movements in the Middle East*, I.B.Tauris, London 1993 pxiii.

make Islam unique and singular. And to ignore the development of secularism in different historical contexts. And to overlook the many changing manifestations of secularism in predominantly Christian countries today.

Sayyid's book is an exasperating read because of the way he remains locked in the very dichotomies he says he wants to deconstruct. He winds up essentialising Islamism in what is really quite an orientalist mode. And to suggest that the only thing Islamist movements respond to is 'the West' is nothing if not 'west-centred'. Once his arguments are stripped of their dense postmodernist jargon they can be seen as being just what he himself most rightly loathes: 'eurocentric'.

The book is also a dismaying read. In countries and communities with strong Islamist tendencies there are brave academics and activists (and they are often both simultaneously) who are struggling on many fronts at the same time: against authoritarian state regimes, patriarchal politics and imperialist encroachment. By his unsympathetic and superficial treatment of them Sayyid adds to the risks they take.

The secular women I studied and worked with in Egypt (and there are countless others like them all over the 'Muslim world') left me in no doubt that their political activism includes the struggle against imperialism. No way would they accept the charge that they imitate 'the West'. They point to long traditions of secular thinking within their own society. When Sayyid writes them off as selling out to 'the West', betraying 'indigenous' movements, he is doing just what he so bitterly blames others for doing. He is countering stereotypes and misconceptions current in 'the West'. But he is doing it by essentialising Islamism, failing to see diversity in it and within 'the West', and ultimately becoming implicated in the destructive process of 'othering' the other. The book leaves me with the disturbing feeling that the eurocentrism Sayyid criticises in others' work is alive and active in his own, having slipped in by the backdoor.

T.V. Sathymurthy 1929 - 1998

We deeply regret to inform our readers that T.V. Sathymurthy, a close associate of the *Soundings* team, died suddenly at his home in York, while a forthcoming article by him for *Soundings* was in the process of being edited.

After nearly thirty years in the Department of Politics at the University of York, Sathya was awarded a Chair shortly before his retirement. His inaugural lecture, 'Labour of Sisyphus, Feast of the Barmecide: the Sentence and the Promise in Development Studies', was at the same time a valediction. 'This is the inaugural lecture, or exordium, from a Personal Chair in Politics about to vanish before our very eyes,' his lecture began.

Sathya was a leading authority on Indian democracy. His edited four-volume study *Social Change and Political Discourse in India* was published by Oxford University Press in 1996. He was a lifelong democrat and socialist, iconoclastic and independent-minded to a fault, whose rigorous academic work was invariably shaped by his deep ethical and political commitments.

He was a great friend of *Soundings*, always supportive of and interested in its project, and sharing its outlook of critical hopefulness towards the present political conjuncture in Britain.

The editors are delighted to announce that there will be a major article from Sathya in the next issue of *Soundings*, especially as its analysis of South Asia breaks new ground for the magazine. It will introduce readers to a subject - the plight and potentialities of democracy in South Asia - which has hitherto received little attention in Britain. We had hoped that Sathya would become a regular contributor to *Soundings*. We are pleased, however, that we will at least be able to publish this fine example of his work in the forthcoming issue.

Windrush echoes

Windrush echoes

On 22 June 1948 the *Empire Windrush* ended its journey from Jamaica by docking at Tilbury and ushering forth 492 people from the Caribbean - most were men, one was a boy of thirteen, and there were no more than twelve women. This event has come to symbolise a process which would transform Britain from its supposed cultural and racial homogeneity into a multi-cultural/multi-racial society. It was to mark the beginning of a long, uneven and contradictory process, in which the UK's long imperial history was to come 'home' in the embodied presence of those who had previously been seen - almost exclusively - solely in pictorial or imaginary form. It was the moment when the meaning of empire for millions of Britons ('host' and 'stranger'/'indigenous' and 'immigrant') began to take on a different reality, as the cauldron of encounter shifted from 'there' to 'here'; it was the beginning of a transformatory process in which

'Still today, less provable, but no less endemic or unjust, forms of discrimination afflict the lives of too many people. In too many walks of life, from Whitehall and the City downward, the glass ceiling is still firmly in place. From personal experience, I know that little more than a decade ago police officers and other Palace of Westminster staff could not believe that an Asian had been elected as an honourable member.' KEITH VAZ, MP

African, Asian and Caribbean migrants – and generations of their descendants – were to construct new narratives of home, new belongings, upon, and alongside, old ones. Of course 1948 does not mark the first presence of people from the Caribbean, Asia, Africa and the Arab world in the UK, as the long-established multi-racial populations of many of the port cities attest. Nor is it the first moment of undoing of a previously culturally homogeneous nation. One only has to remember those groups who had long been in, but never fully encompassed by the national self-image – the Irish and Jewish. To interpret *Windrush* as signalling a beginning in any simple sense is thus only to repeat a series of well established inaccuracies and erasures – inaccuracies and erasures which have been belied in recent years by historical work on black presence in parts of the (ever expanding) Kingdom since at least the late eighteenth century (if not as far back as Elizabethan times).

Despite the erasures and historical inaccuracies which result from the equation of the arrival of the *Windrush* with that of the moment of first arrival of people from the Caribbean, Africa, and Asia, June 1948 does stand for something particular. Of course there is the issue of numerical scale. This date was to mark the beginning of a *mass and permanent* presence of British subjects of a different colour. But there is more to it than this. The presence of diverse peoples from the erstwhile empire was to be at the core of the shifting configurations of 'the nation' and national identity which have been so central in the last four or five decades. When those 492 *British subjects*, many of whom were returned soldiers from the second world war, walked down the gangplanks, they asserted their rights to reside in the 'mother country' and share in its fortunes. Formally the terms of empire gave them every right to do so, but the spatial, social and cultural ordering of empire not did so easily admit of this right. The dis-ease which was to accompany the presence of the 'empire at home' was eventually to reverberate across the national horizon as the process of migration was to widen and deepen into one of multiple immigrations, and

'Yet, we also need to look at the positive side. The Asian community is at the centre of national economic life. We may be told that 'there ain't no black in the Union Jack', but on the football field or the athletics track, there is no lack of brilliant black sportsmen and women proud and overjoyed to play for and represent their country. A sentiment that is heartily reciprocated … The passengers on the *Windrush* were on a voyage of discovery in more ways than one. They were pioneers in the recreation of a diverse, youthful and cosmopolitan nation, whose best days are yet to come.' KEITH VAZ, MP people from the Caribbean, Africa and Asia put down roots across the country. As an iconic moment, then, *The Empire Windrush* is to be seen as representing those multiple diaspora which have helped to change the social, political and cultural topography of the United Kingdom.

But the direction of this changed landscape has been neither linear nor settled. For example, a criminal justice system which allows perpetrators of racist violence and even murder, as in the cases of Stephen Lawrence and Michael Menson, to go undetected and unpunished can persist alongside - even within - a wider socio-cultural environment in which the pains, losses and disgusts of Doreen and Neville Lawrence are embraced and understood as part of a national tragedy.[1] Black athletes and cricketers can be applauded as the finest of the nation at the same time as that nation is depicted in, for example, government white papers on social policy, as almost wholly white and culturally homogenous. Official social and economic data can suggest a profound unevenness in the fortunes of members of what have become 'ethnic minority communities', such that a wider dispersal across all fields of economic and employment opportunity for some, co-exists with persistent un/

'I have been trying to put my mind to what people mean when they say they are British, or that there is a British identity, or that there is a British culture. If indeed there is one, then I must confess that I find it extremely exclusive. There has always been a tremendous diversity within what was perceived to be British, even before the new migration from the Commonwealth - there are clearly very distinct ... identities of Scots, Irish and Welsh ... and even with England there are distinct regional identities ... It is therefore extremely difficult to work out what is considered to be essentially the Britishness of the British. I fear it may have referred to the middle and upper classes from the south of England who have exerted far more influence than those from other parts of the country. They are also the ones who have influenced the image of the British Empire.' BARONESS FLATHER

---

1. This is illustrated by Tony Blair's speech to the Labour Party Conference in September 1998.

under and low paid employment for others.

Within and against these uneven and contradictory processes, diverse populations of African, Asian and Caribbean settlers, and generations of their descendents, have crafted their lives and loves; their families and communities. If these were at times achieved against the odds, it was from these bases that they contributed the economic, political and cultural labours around which what it meant to be 'British' was to be reconfigured. And if the process of reconfiguration struck at the core of what it meant to be white, so too it struck at the core of what it meant to be black, or Asian, or African, or Caribbean. For while white people have been dealt the challenge of facing the destabilisations of what may, in the first fifty years of the century, have felt like psychic and cultural certainties, black people have had to face challenges to their own certainties

'Everything becomes a great deal more complex when we consider the situation of the British-born Asians. Very often the advice at home is 'keep your head below the parapet and concentrate on education, economic success and security'. Is that really going to be sufficient for the new generation? Is that really what it is all about? What about a voice in society? What about being opinion formers?... Six per cent of a very diverse minority population should not be looking for power on the basis of ethnic origin ... that would be as biased as the white majority holding on to it as it is now. But we do need to share in the decision making. And to make sure that whatever such decisions are being taken we are also there to speak for ourselves.' BARONESS FLATHER

which have been born of the arrival of the 'black Briton', and the claims to both the nation and a redefined blackness which this term carries. In this way each of us has been touched by the changes which have been ushered in since June 1948. And it is the pervasive and permanent and unsettled force of these transformations that we have tried to reflect in this special issue of *Soundings*.

The contradictions and tensions which have emerged in the wake of a more diverse and heterogeneous United Kingdom are reflected in each of the contributions which follow. Covering a wide array of issues, and taking many different forms, the pieces also reflect the unsettled and contingent character of contemporary negotiations around 'race', national identity and cultural and political belonging. Ann Phoenix brings these issues to life in her consideration of the shifting boundaries of belonging which young people construct and inhabit. She shows that fixed notions of black/white difference co-exist with more inclusive syncretic forms; she shows that alongside multi-ethnicity there is still much anti-racist work to do.

'A defining "moment" was definitely Enoch Powell's speeches, because almost from that time on I began to feel slightly insecure: maybe not as insecure as many because obviously I've got a good education and I am a professional person, but there is no doubt that I began to think "well hang on, am I someone who is British or am I an immigrant?"' LORD TAYLOR OF WARWICK

This theme of negotiated belonging alongside forms of exclusion is addressed in several of the other pieces. Bilkis Malek uses, among other things, the terrain of football, and more specifically the recent World Cup, to think about the contradictions which have accompanied the development of a destabilised, less secure English identity. She shows how differential responses to 'white' and 'black' violence construct the boundaries and 'essences' of Englishness and how these reflect co-existing processes of inclusion and exclusion. Bilkis Malek ends her piece where Phil Cole begins, by thinking about the implications of globalisation for the development of a more inclusive UK. Phil Cole considers the challenges posed to liberal political theory by processes of global migration and argues that if a more inclusive discursive and policy environment is to be achieved, new notions of citizenship

'... Part of the point about standing as an MP in Cheltenham was breaking the stereotype: I wasn't a footballer, or singer, or a socialist. I was in the Conservative Party ... I wanted to say there are no "no-go" areas, and that black people should be able to stand in Southall or Suffolk: there were these racist boundaries to be broken ... I wanted to encourage black people to think about a new identity, I didn't want us to sleepwalk into the next millennium. I was motivated by pride in the black community. Black people have injected vitality and glamour into British culture and in some respects you could see black people as the saviours of Britain. I think we have a great future.' LORD TAYLOR OF WARWICK and a re-shaped political theory are required.

While only a handful of the travellers on the *Windrush* may have been women, the experiences and contributions of diverse groups of black women have been central to both the changing landscapes of English/Britishness and the meanings of 'blackness' itself. Three of the contributions reflect this. Jackie Kay's short story captures some of the joys, anxieties and disappointments experienced by those black women who were themselves migrants. She uses this fictional form to suggest some of the internal conversations that women of this generation may have had and in so doing gives us some of the flavour of the psychic and emotional

'I suppose a lot of organising in the early days was ... about things having a disproportionate effect on black men – educational exclusion, the 'Sus' laws and so on ... (and) there's a sense in which women felt very comfortable in working on the issue of racism with men, and were also able to be specific about women's issues ... I don't think that men were so comfortable ... I feel that dealing with the complexities and contradictions was easier for women than for men.' BARONESS VALERIE AMOS

consequences of the racialised and gendered division of labour that many black women encountered. But of course, black women were also active architects of their lives in the UK, and Julia Sudbury considers the ways in which diverse constituencies of post-*Windrush* women challenged both the terms of racial exclusion *and* the economies of gender which circulated among sections of the black populations. Challenges to what have often been presented as 'traditional', 'authentic' or 'appropriate' demonstrations of ethnic identity and belonging have been central to the work of black cultural producers over the last two decades. The work of Sonia Boyce has been among the most well-known and in her short photo-essay she captures the instabilities of black gendered identities in a positive statement about self-definition.

If the presence of the *Windrush* generations and their descendents has led to both the destabilisation of 'old' identities and forms of belonging, and to the emergence of new and plural ethnicities, so too has this presence led to transformations in the spatial mappings of the country. This issue is addressed in the photo-essay by Femi Franklin and in the piece by David Sibley. Femi Franklin's pictures and commentary beautifully capture the routes which

Nigerian people established to hold connections between both here and 'home', and families and friends living in different towns around the country. Both this and David Sibley's contribution show the ways in which spaces and places carry racial meanings, and that territorialisation of racial location is linked to wider social and economic processes.

Location then is also a site of ambiguity, negotiation and contestation. This is made apparent in the interview with Simon Hamilton-Clarke and the piece by Roshi Naidoo. As a twelve-year-old boy, Simon Hamilton-Clarke returns to some of the themes addressed more analytically by Anne Phoenix. In particular he shows the contingent character of racialised identities and belongings and clearly expresses the pains associated with racist exclusions. It is from this emotionally painful location that he begins to feel

> '... It's easy to sniff at the idea of role models: I am very resistant to this thing about being put into a representational role, but it has become clearer and clearer that visibility is important. We need people who have power and influence. Communities and young people feel we have a right to be here and a contribution to make in all kinds of ways ... (and) ... I think that it is important for black women to be seen in a range of positions because it's about being seen as having ability in all kinds of different areas.'
> BARONESS VALERIE AMOS

less certain about his claim to a form of Englishness. Yet, as an English boy he also displays many of the sea, sun and sand images that predominate in the British geographical imagination of the Caribbean. It is the common location in contemporary British social and geographical relations, as reflected in the fictional works of diverse migrant/settler communities, that pushes Roshi Naidoo to argue for a collective - i.e. an Asian, African as well as Caribbean - claim to the symbolic significance of *Windrush*. From this position of collective claim more inclusive cultural identities and political constituencies can be produced - ones which can deal with diversity and specificity as much as they can with commonality.

An insistent theme which emerges from many of the contributions is the necessity of both asserting and claiming a black British identity whilst simultaneously maintaining a sense of diasporic connection to other places, identities, communities. An insistence on ethnic identities which are not closed, excluding and fixed, but open, shifting and inclusive. This would mean that just as black people can reconstruct themselves in the confluences of national-international intersections and flows, so too can white people. This is precisely the issue which Val Wilmer addresses in her contribution. She shows how a growing contact and embeddedness in black music led to an ability to remake herself and recognise that she had always been partially formed through encounters with black cultural forms. It is the evidence of the possibility of re-appraising the racial and ethnic character of social, cultural and political landscapes, in this and many of the other

'... If the British-born are rejected and their Britishness not acknowledged they will in turn reject their own identity as British. They will suffer, and are suffering, from a profound sense of loss.' BARONESS FLATHER

'... In using the term Afro-Saxon, I was trying to get black people to think about their identity in a positive way, and it certainly ruffled some feathers: it was about trying to break boundaries.' LORD TAYLOR

'... I would say ... that on the whole we live with ... different kinds of identities quite happily really. I can describe myself as British, as Guyanese, as African, as Caribbean, and I don't have a problem with that because I think that all those describe who I am ... I think part of the difficulty for a lot of people about saying that they are British is about coming to terms with what it means to identify with something that causes pain – racism.' BARONESS VALERIE AMOS

contributions, that leaves space for an optimistic reading of the future shape of a multi-racial/multi-cultural UK. It is equally clear though that there is much still to do in the development of an inclusive and adaptable society, and there are no guarantees as to which direction of pull will win out. What we do know is that the issues which are encapsulated in the symbolism of the *Empire Windrush* are not about to go away, and that first and subsequent generations will continue to plant their Hanging Baskets (in Wood Green and elsewhere) and use them as the source of their offerings to places and peoples that are now 'home'.

'Multicultures', 'multiracisms' and young people

Contradictory legacies of Windrush

Anne Phoenix

Anne Phoenix *looks at the complex approaches both black and white people adopt in making sense of their identities and identifications.*

The fiftieth anniversary of the arrival in Britain, in 1948, of the troopship *Empire Windrush* inspired both celebrations of, and reflections on, the meanings and experiences of Caribbean migration to Britain. The very attention given to the *Windrush* in the British media underlined a crucial change in British society over the last 50 years: from the assumption of monoethnicity to being undeniably and inextricably 'multiracial' and 'multiethnic'. Those who were, in the 1960s (and even in the 1970s), constructed as 'dark strangers' are now represented throughout British society and make crucial contributions both economically and culturally. It is the beneficial nature of these contributions that was a major impetus for the coining of the term 'Cool Britannia' as a new and more useful way to characterise British national identity while giving recognition to its multiethnicity. Alongside changes in media and cultural representations, there have also been changes (although less marked) in research representations. In the last decade, there have also been challenges to research constructions of British African Caribbean people as 'newcomers' and 'outsiders' whose difference from the white majority is inevitably problematic. While such constructions are still common, there are an increasing number of research projects which treat inclusion of people from a variety of ethnic groups as 'normal'.

Yet, while the fiftieth anniversary of the *Windrush* is appropriately cause for celebration and recognition of the dynamism of British society and peoples, it also allows an engagement with the contradictions in this optimistic and romantic story. For the children, grandchildren (and great-grandchildren) of the Windrush generation have not been engaged in straightforward progress from exclusion and being the objects of racism to inclusion and multiculturalism and celebration. Instead, their experiences are, and have been, riven with contradictions of what Phil Cohen has termed 'multicultures' and 'multiracisms'.[1]

This article identifies some of these contradictions as they relate to young people. It argues that, while the pervasiveness of racisms does not constitute an optimistic story, the contradictions between multicultures and multiracisms both open space for disruption of racisms and create a sometimes uneasy and sometimes productive tension between young people's desire for ownership, or sharing, of particular forms of cultural expression and syncretism.

'Multicultures' *and* 'Multiracisms'

It has long been established that the current dynamism and vitality of British cultures have been fuelled by diaspora experience, and the consequences which this has in terms of setting in train processes which unsettle, recombine, hybridise and 'cut-and-mix'. At the same time many who write on culture and racialisation also engage with the theoretical implications of the contradictions between the vibrancy of hybridisation and the pervasiveness of racism. It is, however, less clear how this contradiction is lived out in practice? How do multicultures and multiracisms coexist in young people's daily lives?

---

1. P. Cohen, 'Perversions of Inheritance: studies in the making of multi-racist Britain'. In Cohen, P. and Bains, H. (eds) *Multi-Racist Britain*, Macmillan, London 1988.

Avtar Brah's notion of 'diaspora space' is potentially helpful to the addressing of these questions in relation to the Windrush descendants. As a concept, 'diaspora space' foregrounds both ethnicised and gendered identities. According to Brah, it constitutes the space in which all our genealogies are entangled - those with known histories of migration and those without. It articulates with difference and is the site where diaspora, border and the politics of location intersect. It is, therefore, in 'diaspora space' that the contradictions of multicultures and multiracisms are played out and where binarised categories of racialised and ethnicised belonging and outsider status are reproduced *and* disrupted.[2] These contradictions are an inherent part of 'diaspora space', are part of young people's social geographies and everyday practices.

'Cool Britannia' as ethnically plural and racialised exclusion

Mark Leonard, who coined the term Cool Britannia (once beloved of Tony Blair and other members of the British Labour government), argued that there is a pressing need to renew British identity, and the stagnant image of Britain held in many other countries. Just as British identity was (re)constructed by the Victorians on the basis of its strengths at the time, so, at the end of the twentieth century, Britain needs once more to self-consciously rework British identity. According to Leonard, the current strengths around which a new British identity can be forged include multiculturalism and the major contributions made to the economy and culture by 'minorities'. It would appear, then, that the fiftieth anniversary of *Windrush* finds an indisputable acceptance that the cultural contributions of black and Asian people to British society are now indivisible from British culture - a cultural confirmation of the 1970s slogan 'Come what may, we are here to stay!' Indeed, the economic as well as gastronomic importance of the 'Indian take-away', the 'mainstreaming' of Carnival and of 'black music', are evidence that British identities and cultures are now plural and syncretic.

Yet, whatever the rhetoric of 'multicultures', it still is the case that, when asked, many of the 'British public' give responses which indicate that they do

---

2. A. Brah, *Cartographies of Diaspora*, Routledge, London 1996.
3. See, for example, the surveys commissioned by the Association of Teachers and Lecturers (on schoolchildren) reported in June 1998 and by Operation Black Vote and published in September 1998.

not see British society as indisputably multiethnic.[3] While opinion polls are, in many ways, unsatisfactory measures of attitudes, it does seem that, in practice, it is perfectly possible for 'multicultures' to serve as resources in everyday life while at the same time those who are from ethnic groups other than the white majority continue to be constructed as 'outsiders'. In a study of the identities of young Londoners undertaken by Barbara Tizard and myself, young people gave a variety of accounts about syncretism in youth styles.[4] Some white young people asserted that there were no racialised differences in music or dress:

> I don't think it's directly colour, but I think it's the things, the following and the things that go on - like the way you act and the kind of music you listen to. It's not because you are black, you're white. It's the things that - I mean it's all to do with - it's there for your culture. (Young white woman in group interview).

Others considered that there were racially marked differences in youth style - some of these said that they had, at times, wished to be black in order to be allowed fully to participate in these styles.

> I do sort of remember wishing I was black, so I could sort of be in with the crowd, 'cos I used to sort of be hanging around with a lot of black friends and I was white and sometimes they left me out of it (white young woman).

From most black young people's viewpoints, there were distinctive black and white cultural styles. For some, shared music and dress symbolised unity with other black people and was a powerful focus for identification with blackness as well as a marker of difference from white young people and opposition to racism. Some expressed hostility to white young people who wanted to be part of 'black styles'. This was particularly the case if they considered white entry to black cultural forms to be exploitive appropriation. This tension could be productive in that it spurred on some black young people constantly to create new dance or clothes styles in order to stay 'ahead of', and maintain valued differences

---

4. The study of the Social Identities of 14-18 year old Young Londoners was funded by the Department of Health and conducted at the Thomas Coram Research Unit, Institute of Education.

from, those white young people who wanted to be like them.

Similar contradictions were evident in relation to discourses of racialised exclusion from, or inclusion within, the British nation. For while the young people did not express unitary views, and most black young people considered that they were British, discourses which constructed whiteness as synonymous with Englishness or Britishness were common. Some young people, both black and white, considered that blackness and Englishness were mutually exclusive.

Contradictions of racialised practices

Old ideas do not disappear but, rather, continue to be part of 'accepted wisdom', even as new ideas gain currency; so this contradictory complex of 'multicultures' and 'multiracisms' is hardly surprising. Indeed, work within psychology which focuses on language (e.g. discourse analysis or a rhetorical approach) indicates how readily reconcilable are contradictory racialised practices in everybody's subjectivities. The following example from Michael Billig's work provides a graphic, racialised example of this:

> Immediately after the interview, conducted at school, this young supporter of a racist party, and of compelling all of 'them' to leave 'our country', was to be seen walking arm in arm with a young Asian girl, chatting and laughing in easy friendship.[5]

Billig's example provides an indication that 'multicultures' and 'multiracisms' can simultaneously operate in 'diaspora space' without, apparently, producing any uncomfortable feelings of inconsistency. This fits with the findings of a study of younger children in mainly white primary schools. Troyna and Hatcher concluded that children routinely use both 'hot' (strategic) and 'cold' (non-strategic) interactional strategies, and sometimes deliberately include racist material in their talk with the interactional goal of hurting and, hence, scoring a point. According to Troyna and Hatcher, this 'hot' name-calling occurs regardless of whether children hold racist or actively anti-racist thematic ideologies.[6]

---

5. M. Billig, S. Condor, D. Edwards, M. Gane, D. Middleton and A. Radley, *Ideological Dilemmas: A Social Psychology of Everyday Thinking*, Sage, London 1988, p. 106.
6. B. Troyna and R. Hatcher, *Racism in Children's Lives: A study of mainly-white primary schools*, Routledge, London 1992.

This ability to sustain contradiction in racialised practices was repeatedly evident in the Social Identities study. Almost all the young people interviewed espoused a strongly egalitarian discourse, in which they argued that everybody was equal and should be treated equally, regardless of 'race', gender and social class. However, many also recognised that there was informal segregation in their schools, as is evident in the quote below from a group interview with ethnically mixed 16- and 17-year-old young women attending an all girls' school.

Q.   *Can I ask now about friendships ... and whether you have a wide range of friends?*
A1.   It doesn't matter what colour, race or religion your friends are. I mean you should be friends with them for what they are, not what they look like or (inaudible).

Q.   *So what colour are your friends in school?*
A1.   Everything. Someone's colour doesn't matter to me...
A2.   Everyone has said that everyone has got black friends, they've got Turkish friends, they've got all sorts of friends, but when it comes down to it - when you are sitting in assembly, when you're sitting in a big room, there's always the people that stick together. There's the black people. There's the white people.
A3.   Especially in school.
A4.   That is true.

All speak simultaneously – loud and heated but not clear.
A.   Like even in that room outside, there's like all one group sitting on one side and all the others sitting on the other side. I mean they'll talk to each other and they're friends. I'm not saying they don't talk to each other and ignore each other, but it's just there.

Given that young people are differentiated by the 'youth styles' they occupy, it is perhaps not surprising that there is some informal racialised segregation in most schools simply on that basis. In a study of the masculinities of 11-14 year old boys,[7]

---

7.   This study is currently being conducted by Stephen Frosh, Ann Phoenix and Rob Pattman and is funded by the Economic and Social Research Council, grant number L129251015.

some boys claimed that there is more racism among the 11-year-olds who have just started secondary school than among the 14-year-olds. At the same time, they argued that there is 'less mixing' among the 14-year-olds. According to these narratives, 11-year-olds mix more because they are finding their place in school hierarchies; whereas 14-year-olds have established their hierarchies and can, therefore, be egalitarian, while only mixing with those with whom they feel a degree of shared cultural style.

It is not however the case that informal segregation (which is commonly reported in London schools) solely results from differences in youth styles. Indeed, informal segregation is itself contradictory. It limits the syncretism possible, since it reduces opportunities for joint cultural production. And it also allows racisms and mutual suspicion quietly to flourish. Yet, in an atmosphere where some white young people and black young people are mutually wary of each other, they are also reflexive about the contradictions, and pervasiveness, of racialisation. Their accounts provided rationalisations of informal segregation which varied according to their racialised positions:

Q.   *Why are you more comfortable with black people?*

A.   Well I have got a lot more in common with black people because I don't know anything about the whites ... and what I do know I don't like, so I wouldn't really be comfortable.

Q.   *What do you know that you don't like?*

A.   Well you know - about the racism that is going on, so you know I wouldn't really be comfortable going - because when you go into a room and it is full of white people you don't personally know which one of them is racist or if they are racist. There is a doubt in your mind whether they are going to be racist or not, so you know, until you get to - until I get to know a person, a white person, I don't really - so it takes that bit of time. So I wouldn't really be comfortable unless I know what they are like or how they are (black young woman).

Q.   *Do you feel more comfortable with white people or black people or does it make no difference?*

A.   It makes no difference. But when there are a group of black people I do feel, they seem to, they like, I do feel pressurised. I feel very uncomfortable because they seem to resent - not you being white, but I just think if they're in a group then they must feel pressurised, or I think to myself why do they all go round in a group? And sometimes I feel slightly threatened because they must be angry that they feel an outcast. I mean surely they must think of themselves and go - you know- go in a group with all black people and I resent that. And if you walk past you think, oh you know - I don't know - you just - you get vibes from them and you do feel threatened slightly (white young woman).

Informal segregation is not, of course, the only story to be told about racialisation in schools. A feature of 'multicultures' in Britain and the US is the marked increase there has been in the numbers of people of 'mixed-parentage' and in 'mixed' relationships and friendships - some of which are forged at school. However, informal segregation serves to highlight the differentiation of young people's racialised experiences. It also confirms that mixed schooling is not guaranteed to produce any more familiarity and understanding between different ethnicities than it has done between genders.

'Multicultures' and 'multiracisms': so what?

From all the above examples, it seems clear that understandings of the contradictions of 'multicultures' and multiracisms' can only be advanced through an engagement with people's own subjective understandings, constructed through their racialised narratives. Simply knowing whether they are white or black, or which schools they go to, tells us little about their positioning within 'diaspora space'.

It might be argued that the contradictions discussed above may be interesting, but they are hardly consequential. After all, social life is riven with contradictions and the Windrush legacy has allowed young people (black and white) to create plural identities, drawing on a range of cultures to do so. However, the 50 years since the *Windrush* arrived in Britain have also been marked by a proliferation of racisms. The repercussions of this are most evident in racist murders such as that of the 18-year-old black young man, Stephen Lawrence, in 1994. More prosaically, they are also evident in the proliferation of racist discourses, and in the ease with which racist name-calling is evoked as a powerful weapon among children and young people. For example, the working-class white young people (particularly young men) studied by Roger Hewitt produced unashamedly racist discourses, which blamed black people for the economically impoverished circumstances in which the white participants in the study lived.[8]

There has been a backlash against antiracism (on the grounds that it is a dictatorial form of political correctness); and recognition of the complexity of racisms, and the difficulties posed by essentialist conceptions of 'race' and racisms, has made some anti-racist positions untenable; but it continues to be important to confront racisms, while recognising the contradictions and the dynamism of racialisation, and that these contradictions are always expressed through subjectivities.

It may well be that the very contradictions of 'multicultures' and 'multiracisms' can allow space for the disruption of multiracisms. Antaki and Widdicombe argue that social life is 'a continuous display of people's local understandings of what is going on', and that ... 'identity is used in talk: something that is part and parcel of the routines of everyday life, brought off in the fine detail of everyday interaction.'[9]

However, identities are not simply resources to be used in talk; they are also produced through talk - in the narratives we tell ourselves and others:

> We achieve our personal identities and self-concept through the use
> of the narrative configuration, and make our existence into a whole
> by understanding it as an expression of a single unfolding and developing
> story. We are in the middle of our stories and cannot be sure how they will
> end; we are constantly having to revise the plot as new events are added to
> our lives. Self, then, is not a static thing or a substance, but a configuring of
> personal events into an historical unity which includes not only what one has
> been but also anticipations of what one will be.[10]

---

8. R. Hewitt, *Routes of Racism*, Centre for Multicultural Education, Institute of Education, London 1996.
9. C. Antaki and S. Widdicombe, 'Identity as an achievement and as a tool', C. Antaki and S. Widdicombe (eds), *Identities in Talk*, Sage, London 1998.
10. D.Polkinghorne, *Narrative Knowing and the Human Sciences*, State University of New York, Albany 1988, 150.

It is therefore crucially important that local understandings, produced in the narratives of everyday talk, are engaged with as the site in which it is possible to disrupt racisms.

Phil Cohen argues that the young white working-class people he studied attributed the deterioration of their circumstances and neighbourhoods to the black people who had increasingly come to live in the same neighbourhoods:

> It is possible to glimpse here how autobiographies are re-written according to a racist grammar in contexts where the links between growing-up-working-class are getting harder and harder to make in any real terms.[11]

That it is possible to re-write autobiographical narratives lends support to the idea that it is not helpful to think of people in terms as fixed and polarised as racist or not racist; instead attention should be given to racist or anti-racist discourses. The quote from Phil Cohen is, arguably, an optimistic one, since, if it is possible to rewrite autobiographical narratives in a more racist direction, it must also be possible to rewrite them in an anti-racist direction. But the ways in which it might be possible to provide the resources for children and young people to do this are not straightforwardly clear. Nevertheless, as Roger Hewitt argues in *Routes of Racism*, engagement with what young people actually say when expressing racist discourses is likely to be a first step. At the same time, opposition to racism is also crucially important, as this quote from a secondary school teacher illustrates:

> I have always thought that my white liberalism was emblazoned all over me, but I will never forget the response of a black girl, whom I had taught for two years, to an outburst of mine condemning racists. She simply said 'I never knew you were one of us miss', because she had missed all the subtle responses and statements I had ever made concerning prejudice.[12]

As a descendant of the Windrush generation, I have welcomed the media's

---

11. P. Cohen, *Rethinking the Youth Question*, MacMillan, London 1997, p. 162.
12. B. Hunter, M. Simons and J. Stephens, 'Teaching against racism: literature and knowledge', *The English Magazine*, 13, 5-11, 1984, p. 10.

marking of the event as one of celebration, and the representation of black British people as multifaceted, and as having agency, rather than as passive victims or incomprehensible outsiders. However, the fiftieth anniversary is also quietly commemorated by those who seek new ways of representing the ways in which we are all connected in 'diaspora space' because of the Windrush event (and the historic relations which fashioned it). The representations which result from analysis of the contradictions and complexities of multicultures and multiracisms are a notable legacy of the *Windrush*. More such representations are needed to disrupt multiracisms and to celebrate multicultures as both shift and change, in ways we cannot yet imagine, over the next fifty years.

An earlier version of this paper was presented at the Institute of Education, University of London, as part of the spring seminar series organised by the Centre for New Ethnicities Research, on 'Race, Education and the "Multicultural"Society'.

Out of hand

Jackie Kay

Today has the unmistakable quality to it. Definitely a hand-day. She may as well write the day off because she knows it is out of hand the minute she wakes and stares at them. That will be her till bedtime. Sitting, looking, is not an unpleasant way to pass the day. And there is not a lot she can do about it.

Rose McGuire Roberts holds her hands up to the light, turns them, this way and that. There are things hands can do happily; there are things hands instinctively disdain. Sometimes life gets out of hand. Her hands with their long beautiful fingers (so she used to be told). Her hands with her half moon nails, quite pink. Smooth, black, aching, memorable hands: dark life line, dark heart line, small lighter branches of children waving at the edge of her palm. Somebody counted six once when she was young; six children bending round the side of her hand. Thank God they didn't know what they were talking about. Fifty years ago, these were the hands that clapped, then came to England. Willing.

Twenty-six years old they were then. In their prime with their nails filed and shining. No calcium spots. No loose skin. No wrinkles on the back of themselves. Twenty-six year old hands. Dancing hands, talking hands, story hands, moving, working hands. On the go the whole time, rarely still, rarely silent. Twenty-six years old, they arrived, elegant, black, skilled, beautiful hands. Ready and willing. Ready was the left hand; willing the right. What a thing for a hand to get to do. What a way to tend a hand. They held onto the ship's cold rail full of their own sense of importance. She rubbed them together and told them to stop shaking. She gripped one onto the other to stop the trembling excitement. To stop her hands flapping into flighty birds. To contain herself. Her breathing was fast. Her chest tight with anticipation. England, England, England! Here she comes!

Fifty years ago, hand over heart, Rose McGuire Roberts stepped off the Windrush with her good hands, her dab hands, her handy hands.

Many hands make light work

Today is a hand-day. They just come up, days like this, and grab her from nowhere. She is propelled into her favourite seat to sit and think and contemplate her hands. And the more she thinks, the more she sees. Her daughter rushes about forgetting herself. Her grandchildren sit in front of computers all day long, pressing buttons and killing people. Pow! Gotcha! Bad! Snide! Her son is so concerned about money, he hardly sees her. He could lose quite a bit of money just sitting chatting to his mother and having dinner. When he does come, he gets out one of those mobile phones and spends quite a portion of the time swearing at the battery which is always running out. So that's family. Her husband, Alexander, is dead. Dead and buried in the wrong country. That's life. They always talked, Alexander and she, of going back; but somehow it stayed just talk. Lots of talk. But talk just the same. And a strange thing started to happen in these talks with Alexander; it was like the pair of them were just imagining their country. The images got so vivid maybe they were afraid to go back. If it was a disappointment - what then?

So she is just sitting. Let everybody else rush, rush. Let them all think their rushing is important. Running rushing feet. Let them run round London up and down the escalators, in and out of the city like mad dogs. She sucks her lips and makes a sound that she is still teaching her twin granddaughters. They are quite good at it you know. Surprising.

Fifty years in England and look at the change in her hands. They are still her hands; she can recognise them. But they are wrinkled on the back of themselves and swollen between her knuckles. And one of them, the right one, the willing one, is giving her quite a bit of bother. She can't use it properly: hold a pen, or a duster, turn a knob or twist a bottle top, clean her glasses, whisk an egg. Actually if a person were to look only at her hands they would think that she was older than seventy-six. Her face looks younger. Everybody says so. 'You don't look seventy-six, you know.' 'Don't I now?' she says. 'Well, I don't feel like any spring chicken.' She likes that expression – 'spring chicken.' 'Oh yes,' they'll say, 'You don't look sixty-five if you are a day.' 'If you are a day,' she repeats to herself. 'If you are a day.' Like she should be pleased. What's the matter with looking seventy-six., what's the matter with looking eighty? But she is pleased, a little. If she admits it. Pleased her face is smooth with hardly a wrinkle.

Her hands are older than her face. That is the simple truth of the matter. Almost as if they came into the world a good five years earlier than she did and were hanging around disembodied, picking things from trees and stroking smooth materials, snapping their fingers and sucking their thumbs until the rest of her came along and they found themselves attached. Perhaps they did have a life of their own for a while. The thought is a comfort. Because once they came to England they certainly had no life of their own! At all at all at all.

Rose McGuire Roberts came down those Windrush steps. She already felt the moment momentous as she was doing so. Step by step and staring down into the waiting crowd.

Tilbury didn't look like England. A dock is a dock. There were people waiting to greet the boat, waving, welcoming. It was quite something. The ones waiting and the ones coming off. The willing hands. It was June. She never forgets the date: June 22, 1948.

It takes her a week to find a room. She dumps her heavy suitcase down and lines the drawer with paper so she has somewhere clean for her clothes. The room is sad and unfriendly like the landlady. But she is not yet discouraged. Things will pick up. She can make the room cheerful. Maybe she can make the landlady cheerful. Rose opens her door and Mrs Bleaney opens her door further down the stairs. Her head peeps out. (She was to see this nosey head peeping out many times in the next couple of years.) 'Going out are you?' 'I'm going to the cinema,' Rose says bubbling. 'The cinema, are you? Already? Don't be late back. I lock the door early.'

Rose McGuire Roberts sits herself down in the red seat. England, she is in England. She is in the cinema in England! How about that? Wait till she writes home to tell her mother. I wasted no time! The day I found my lodgings, I went to the cinema! Before *The Treasure of the Sierra Madre*, there is the Pathé news. And to Rose's absolute astonishment and disbelief, there she is up on the cinema on the news! It is herself right enough, coming off that ship. 'Last week in Tilbury 494 Jamaicans came ashore from the Empire Windrush. They have come to help the British economy. Many of them feel like they are coming home. Hundreds of people were gathered at Tilbury together. Welcome Home. Welcome Home.' Rose sees herself for a brief moment in black and white coming down the ship's steps with her red hat on. (Though only she knows it is red.) Her hat is tilted to the side and she is holding onto it. Her coat has blown open a bit and her smart navy dress is showing. She'd like to lean forward to the people in the seat in front of her and shout, 'That's me, that's me. That hat is red, that dress is navy. I know the colours she is wearing. She is me!' She watches herself come down the steps with the other willing hands. For a moment, sitting there on her red seat, she feels the false shyness of a movie star. Didn't the person in front of her recognise her and turn round and stare? She'll have to watch out. At the end of *The Treasure of the Sierra Madre*, people might be asking her for her autograph! She practised it enough times before getting on the Windrush. People's handwriting in England will be very neat, she had thought to herself. Neat and elegant. English. English handwriting.

After the Pathé news, the movie begins. Rose leans forward in her seat. She has got a bag of sweets. She will wait till it is slap bang in the middle of the movie before she opens this bag of sweets. She strains to see the time on her watch in the dark cinema. She is all cosy, safe. 'The movie was all about three losers searching for gold,' she imagines writing to her little sister back in Jamaica. 'Humphrey Bogart was the star. Do you know who Humphrey Bogart is? They might get rich but they don't get lucky.'

People start leaving the movie before the credits are finished. A lot of people stare at her as they leave. They definitely recognised her! No question! Only the stare is not friendly like you would expect. Well, maybe they are jealous! Maybe they wanted to be on the Pathé news! She sits and waits till every name has been and gone on the screen. When the credits finally finish, she is the only one left in the cinema. What an experience.

Rose gets up and goes out into the tactless daylight. A little dizzy. It is a nasty shock after the cinema's chocolate darkness.

Rose McGuire Roberts can remember everything about those first few weeks in England in vivid colours. The red buses, red pillar boxes, red phone booths. The yellow jacketed underground men. The green green grass. When was it exactly it started to change? After two weeks? Just two weeks?

She is a skilled nurse. Highly qualified. In Jamaica she was the youngest ward sister in the hospital. At Westminster Hospital, she is put on night shift. She stays on night-shift for two years, even though she keeps trying to get off it. The night hangs to her back; she can't escape it. Well, she never minded hard work. It's not the hard work that's the problem. It's the fact that she's been landed all the rubbish jobs, all the jobs she shouldn't be doing. Making tea, emptying rubbish, turning the patients in the night from left side to right on her own, cleaning the bed pans. Somehow she ends up with all the bed-pans to empty. Now how did that happen? Is she imagining the smile on the other nurses' faces? Is she imagining that sly satisfied look?

That was the beginning of it, Rose thinks to herself looking at her hands. The back and the front. The right and the left. Old now, definitely. Old and vulnerable looking. When she was young she never imagined that hands would age along with the rest of you and that it would upset her so. Well you don't imagine age at all when you are young. Look at her twin granddaughters now. When she tells them about herself as a young woman, they think she is making it up! They think she is lying! As far as her twin granddaughters are concerned she has always been the old fat woman that she is right now. It is just as impossible for them to imagine her young as it was all those years ago to imagine herself ever getting old.

All the bed pans in the world for her. Her willing hands. Emptying the steel pans with the terrible crunched bits of tissue in them and the strong smelling stools of the very ill. Well not so much stools as pouffes! Not even pouffes, pillows. Burst pillows! Explosions! That is better. English explosions! Night shift at Westminster hospital. Patients in the night are frightened. They shout out, restless. They want their mothers even if they are old women and men. They fear death is going to come and snatch them away. Sometimes death does come in the night with its long scratchy fingers to claim somebody. The white curtain gets pulled sharply round the round rail. The worried patient in the bed next door wakes to see the terrifying white curtain, the final curtain. The shuffling and whispering goes on. The thudding movements. In the morning, just before Rose goes off her shift, the patients stare at the empty bed, appalled. Once a woman shouts at her. 'You there! It's all your fault. You've brought your strange diseases with you! None of us would be in here if it weren't for you.'

What is so awful is not the nutcase of the woman who is shouting at her, but the fact that her fellow nurses are smiling in the weak daylight. The fact that not one of them does a single thing to help. Nobody tries to shut the woman up, so she continues. 'Practising your strange ways here, your black magic!' she screams.

Rose would have liked to wash her hands of the whole country right then and there. Because nobody took the woman in hand. Nobody got high-handed with her and said, 'Now now Mrs Wells that's quite enough!' Rose McGuire's twenty-six-year-old hands longed to slap the woman right across her face. To shout, 'Don't be so nasty!' She felt her skin burn.

And it wasn't just the one woman she had problems with. She was just the tip of the iceberg. She would never tell her twin granddaughters about all that now. She doesn't want them to know. She didn't even tell her own children.

The next one, if she remembers right, was a man with a pinched face and a sharp irritable nose. Just as she was turning him over, he whispered hoarsely in her ear, go back to the jungle. She carried the sound of his fierce whisper all the way home. And home wasn't all that different because the landlady there had a look on her face that said more or less the same thing. And it got so bad at one stage that Rose could no longer tell which people had the look on their face and which didn't. That's how bad it got. It was difficult for her to trust anybody being nice. If somebody was nice, Rose would wonder why they were being nice. She never used to wonder that. She never used to carry this suspicion around with her under her tongue, sucking on it, like a poisonous sweet.

So what did she do? She went to the movies. Half the time she fell asleep in the cinema because of the night shift. She'd hear *The Secret Life of Walter Mitty* in the background and think dozily to herself, 'Is that him telling another lie again?' *It's a Wonderful Life, The Red Shoes, Rope,* Lauren Bacall in *The Florida Keys. Give My Regards to Broadway* in technicolor, Bogart and Bacall again in *Key Largo,* Rita Hayworth with her pretty auburn hair bleached in the gripping, *The Lady from Shanghai.* 'It's true, I made a lot of mistakes,' Rita says in her dying breath. Rose watches Olivia De Havilland go crazy in *The Snake Pit.* Joan Fontaine in *Letter from an Unknown Woman.* Joan Fontaine has beautiful hands, Rose thinks to herself, stylish. James Cagney in *White Heat.* 'Top of the world, Ma' shrieks Cagney as he goes up in flames! Everybody is losing their mind, Rose thinks to herself, at home in the movies.

And one day. One day Rose McGuire Roberts stopped going to the movies. She came out of the cinema in 1958, a hot August day, with her husband, the year of the Nottingham riots, she came out of the cinema and a group of white people gathered round them and shouted, 'Go back to your own country.'

This is the question she asks herself the most on these hand-days. How come she thought England was her country? How did that happen? How was it that she thought when she got on that Windrush that she was coming home?

It is late in the evening. The river is running slow. She closes her curtains. She hand washes her pants. She gets into bed. Even having a family didn't take away that lonely feeling. Because nobody knew. And her husband was a cheerful man. Don't dwell on it Rose, it'll eat you up, he'd say. Don't dwell on it. But the thing about these hand-days are the more she dwells, the better she feels. Oh no! Never tell people to just forget it. She has got to remember. She can see herself on a big screen. Red hat. Navy dress. Coming down off the Windrush. She could almost applaud. Was that some other girl? No it wasn't. It was herself. Rose MeGuire Roberts coming off that huge fiction of a ship. Stepping.

Hidden struggles
*Black women's activism
and black masculinity*

Julia Sudbury

Julia Sudbury *looks at the complexity and the
differences between the lives of black women and
those of black men.*

As we celebrate the long hard struggle represented by the fiftieth anniversary
of the landing of the *Empire Windrush*, another less feted anniversary is about
to pass by unnoticed. Twenty years ago, black women from Africa, the Caribbean
and Asia launched OWAAD, the Organisation of Women of African and Asian
Descent. OWAAD was conceived of as an umbrella organisation which would
bring together black women as individuals and community activists from all
over the United Kingdom, to campaign against injustices facing the black
community at large, as well as issues facing black women in particular. Black
women who participated in OWAAD, as well as in the black women's
organisations which sprung up in every location with a substantial black
population, from the late 1970s to the mid 1980s, began to develop
understandings of the ways in which black women's experiences of racism were
distinct from those of black men. When they looked at racist immigration
legislation and practice, they also highlighted the ways in which those practices
discriminated in specific ways against women - as in the 'virginity tests' which
many women from the Indian subcontinent were subjected to at Heathrow
airport. When they looked at racism in the National Health Service, they also
identified the widespread practice of prescribing Depo Provera, a long-term
contraceptive with damaging side effects, to black women, and pointed to the
racist construction of black women's sexuality as a key component in their

oppression. In other words, black women activists began to identify the ways in which 'race' is also, always, gendered.

Black women's attempts to understand these complex intersections of race, class and gender sometimes resulted in overly simplified cumulative approaches which viewed black women as triply oppressed and therefore 'worse off' than both black men and white women. Adding sexism to racism and class exploitation seemed to offer an explanation for black women's location at the bottom of the socio-economic pile. However, it also led to a rigid political perspective in which black men and women, straight and lesbian, were ranked in a hierarchy of oppressions which left little room for an analysis of situations which did not fit this theoretical framework. For example, it failed to look at the ways in which black young people, both men and women, were stigmatised and excluded. At its best, however, black women engaged in grassroots theorising produced more nuanced understandings, which looked at the ways in which race, class and gender were articulated to form complex and fluid outcomes. Without losing sight of the brutal forms which racialised sexism could take in black women's lives, from sterilisation to violent attacks in the home, black women theorised the intersection of systems of dominance in ways which left open the possibility that black women would not always, everywhere, be found at the bottom. Rather than the winner/loser perspective of the hierarchy of oppression approach, this new approach challenged us to ask more complex questions and to seek more nuanced answers.

The need for more complex questions is perhaps exemplified by recent newspaper headlines which proclaimed that even as we celebrate the bitter-sweet memory of those men lining the decks of the *Windrush*, 'Black women have overtaken ... black men in the pay stakes' . Based on recent research by the Employment Policy Institute, which found that African Caribbean women earned more per hour on average than both black men and white women, these headlines simply brought to mainstream attention folk-knowledge which has circulated within the African Caribbean communities for over five years. African Caribbean women, the argument goes, are leaving their men behind. Concentrating on individual educational and professional advancement rather than the 'manly' pursuits of rebellion, resistance and community defence, black women are embraced by a society scared of those 'angry' black men, yet fearful also of appearing racist.

I think we're in danger of leaving everybody behind that is not compromising. Which is why I think so many black women are leaving their men behind. I never thought as a dyke I'd be worried about this. But I am seriously, genuinely worried about what is happening to black men in this country ... I think what's happening is that straight black women are ... making it, you can see them, they're the first ones as Assistant Director in the voluntary sector.

Perusal of the black press reveals numerous allusions to the assumption that African Caribbean women are doing better than 'our men' (*The Voice* 23.4.96, 5.3.96, 26.3.96). This supposed differential is attributed to the idea that while black men are a threat to white men and women, black women are more acceptable.

Black women's advancement is never seen as beneficial to the black community as a whole. Conservative councillor Lola Ayonride states:

EOPs have helped black or African women to get highly paid jobs ... But in the process, our men have lost out' ... 'There has been enough talk about the African woman, now let us deal with the African man. They are threatened with extinction. A successful black woman without a successful black man has nothing to be proud of'.[1]

The argument that black men are under attack is given further support by evidence of police brutality, imprisonment, massive unemployment and the proliferation of guns and drugs, all of which suggest that African Caribbean men in Britain are sliding down the slope of American style 'ghetto' deprivation.[2]

The argument that black men suffer more in a system of racialised oppression is of course not a new one. It was a feature of black nationalist ideologies of the 1960s, and led to the alienation of many black women from organisations such as RAAS, and Black Power groups in Britain, as well as the Black Panthers and SNCC in the US. Black women who formed the first autonomous organisations in the late 1970s and early 1980s faced hostility from many black men, who

---

1. Cited in Z. Yeebo, 'Now is the time to save the African Man from extinction', in *The African* 1, African Development Communications Network, London 1995, p29.
2. See Z. Yeebo, as in note 1.

believed that by calling attention to sexism and violence within black communities they were colluding with the racist stigmatisation of black men, and distracting attention from the 'real' issues such as police brutality, economic exclusion and political marginalisation.

Images of black female betrayal and black male emasculation draw on a long history of racialised relations in the Black Atlantic. They build on collective memories of slavery and the belief that women's position was ameliorated by their ability to manipulate the master enslaver's sexual attention in order to win better treatment. They also draw on popular representations of the female 'house slave' who was able to wear fancy 'hand-me-downs' and eat left-over food from the master's table, while the enslaved men worked in the fields and plotted revenge and flight:

> There is a strongly held opinion that ... black women have always been sexually liberated. This argument has its foundations in slavery and is based on the so-called 'easy' life of those black women who were forced to 'service' their white masters sexually. Their condition has historically been projected as being closer to that of white women than black men[3]

Such depictions were steeped in sexism and have since been countered by more accurate representations of the sexual coercion and rape to which enslaved women were subject, the involvement of the vast majority in gruelling work in the fields and the role of maroon and enslaved women in resistance to the enslavers in America and the Caribbean.[4]

The idea that enslaved African women were given favours by the master enslavers finds its parallel in the notion that women of African descent are progressing because white males allow them to. In this sense, African

---

3. Brixton Black Women's Group, 'Black Feminism', in H. Kanter, S. Lefanu, S. Shah, C. Shedding (eds) in *Sweeping Statements: Writings from the Women's Liberation Movement 1981-83*, Women's Press, London 1984, p251.
4. See A. Davis, *Women, Race and Class*, The Women's Press, London 1981; B. Bush, 'Defiance or Submission? The Role of the Slave Woman in Slave resistance in the British Caribbean', in D.C. Hine, W. King and L. Reed (eds) 'We Specialize in the Wholly Impossible': *A Reader in Black Women's History*, Carlton Publishing, New York 1995.

Caribbean women are seen as 'selling out' the black community. 'Selling out' does not necessarily involve taking political positions which actively undermine black community interests. Simply by exceeding the economic and educational achievements of their menfolk, African Caribbean women are seen as contributing to the former's emasculation and thus to white domination. While economic power in the hands of men is seen as empowering the community, such power in the hands of African Caribbean women is seen as a threat to African Caribbean masculinity and therefore to community cohesion. To a large extent this rhetoric draws on black nationalist discourse from the United States.[5]

The implications of such beliefs are clear. Black women who attain professional positions or reasonably paid employment are chastised for 'emasculating' their menfolk or being disloyal to 'the community'; while those who remain in low paid exploitative work, or fail to find stable employment, simply become invisible. The implication for political activism by black women is also clear. Black women's autonomous activism begins to lose its legitimacy. Black women are expected to focus their attention not on the problems of racism, brutality and poverty facing black women, but on the exclusion, criminalisation and violence enacted against black boys and men.

In this context data such as that published by the Employment Policy Institute, and the headlines it produces, enter a discursive sphere overlain with ideas of betrayal and collusion, privilege and 'emasculation'. Folk beliefs about gender relations in African Caribbean communities prevent an adequate interrogation of the new findings. Thus suggestions that the survey overlooked other factors affecting the statistics on black women's wage rates were given little attention, in either black or mainstream presses. But there have been interrogations of the findings: for instance the survey overlooked geographical disparities such as the predominance of black women in urban areas like London, where wages are higher; it also ignored the higher rates of female activity in informal sectors such as homeworking, which fail to show up in surveys.

African Caribbean women enter a labour market which is gendered as

---

5. See, for example, N. Hare and J. Hare *The Endangered Black Family: Coping with the Unisexualization and Coming Extinction of the Black Race*, Black Think Tank, San Francisco 1984.

well as racialised. They are concentrated in 'women's jobs' - low and intermediary level jobs within the service and public sectors - such as clerical work, nursing, cleaning and childcare.[6] When unemployment data from the 1991 census on African and Caribbean communities are disaggregated, other patterns begin to appear. Not only do African men and women experience higher unemployment rates than Caribbean men and women (27.0 to 18.9 per cent), but African women actually experience slightly higher unemployment rates than Caribbean men (24.7 to 23.8 per cent). Even the relatively superior employment prospects of Caribbean women must be put in context of an unemployment rate of over double that of white women (13.5 to 6.3 per cent).[7] And in the light of the increased burdens of childcare and household costs which fall on those African Caribbean women who have no financial contribution from a male partner, it is also likely that the relative advantage for Caribbean women in escaping unemployment will be undermined by problems of stress, overwork and exhaustion. Furthermore, their concentration in low status professions such as nursing, and in 'race' specific jobs, such as Section 11 posts in the welfare and education sectors, further undermines this apparent mobility, and increases black women's vulnerability to government cuts, and changes in policy such as moves away from 'race specific' funding initiatives.

W hile the Employment Policy Institute findings do little to elucidate the continuing problems facing black women, they have served to bring to the surface a simmering debate about black male-female parity. While black women have long struggled for racial equality between blacks and whites, as well as gender equality between black men and women, anti-racist activists have frequently succumbed to gender-blind race thinking in which demands are made for racial parity even as gender inequality is normalised. Data which suggests that black women may begin to exceed black male progress in some areas shakes expectations that removing racism will enable black men to take their 'rightful' place at the head of the household. As more black women progress into professional and managerial positions, black men will need to

---

6. See R. Bhavnani, *Black women and the Labour Market: A Research Review*, Equal Opportunities Commission, Manchester 1994.
7. D. Owen, *Ethnic Minority Women and the Labour Market: Analysis of the 1991 Census*, Equal Opportunities Commission, Manchester 1994.

interrogate their visions for an anti-racist future, and question whether that future is necessarily one in which equality for black males is achieved through the reinscription of unequal gender relations.

Rethinking anti-racist activism

What hope then is there for meaningful coalitions between black women and black men around a holistic agenda for social change? My own work suggests that there are four areas where the potential for coalition building is present, or where such coalitions are beginning to emerge, often in embryonic form.[8]

The first area is the emergence of a number of progressive initiatives focusing on black men in London, Birmingham and Manchester. There are organisations which aim to re-think black masculinity, to question 'macho' behaviour, and to counter violence against black women and children. In London the Black Male Forum hosts debates on gender relations within the African Caribbean community. The Black Fathers Project explores the ways in which parenting by African, Asian and Caribbean men is affected by racism, sexism and the pressure to conform to traditional family roles. In Manchester, Kemetic Educational Guidance organises study sessions for African Caribbean men in prison, with an emphasis on analysing the roots of abusive behaviour, and embracing 'African centred' values such as respect for women. In Birmingham, the Rites of Passage programme creates a learning environment for male teenagers to prevent destructive behaviour and challenge sexist notions of African Caribbean women as 'baby mothers'.

While the male leadership of these organisations is nothing new, these initiatives are unique in their overt focus on black masculinity, their acknowledgement of the specificity of black male experience and their willingness to acknowledge destructive patterns of behaviour by black men. This indicates two significant changes in the approach to community activism by black men. Firstly, there is an acknowledgement for the first time that black men's experience is not 'The Black Experience', and that autonomous and focused organisation by both black men and women is valid. Rather than viewing black women's autonomy as 'splitting the community', these organisations embrace the notion

---

8. J. Sudbury *'Other Kinds of Dreams': Black Women Organising*, Routledge, London 1998.

of organising on the basis of gendered experiences of racism and community. Secondly, these approaches differ dramatically from the insistence by many black male leaders on not 'airing dirty linen':

> I have been told many times by elders who should know better, that there are certain things about the Black communities which we must conceal, that must not be talked about, because to reveal them would be to fuel the fires of racism and state oppression. We must close ranks at whatever cost.[9]

This closure has meant keeping a veil of silence over sexism and abuse within black communities. For the first time, it is black men who are exploring problems within black communities, and the impact of racism in reinforcing these problems. In overturning two stalwarts of opposition to black women's autonomy, these organisations appear to pave the way for effective partnership with black women activists.

A second arena of successful coalitions between black men and women has been the development of black voluntary sector umbrella organisations. At the local level, umbrella groups such as the Black Community Forum in Sheffield, the Ethnic Community Forum in Cambridge, Bath Network of Black Organisations and Bristol Black Voluntary Sector Development Unit have been established throughout the 1980s and 1990s. These forums have active involvement from black women's organisations. Several women whom I interviewed stated that their political concerns at the local level were channelled through these bodies, as they were less easily singled out for punitive action by local authorities. Support was also received when funding was cut or threatened.

The introduction of 'partnership' funding, involving group bids from statutory, voluntary and private sectors, is gradually changing the face of voluntary sector funding. It is clear that if black women's organisations are to receive any funds from such initiatives, they will be forced to form coalitions with other black organisations. Attempting to negotiate as an individual organisation, when large corporations are sitting at the table with

---

9. H. Bains, 'Southall Youth: an Old Fashioned story', in P. Cohen and H. Bains (eds) *Multi-racist Britain*, Macmillan Press, Basingstoke and London 1988, p226.

their eye on million pound 'flagship' schemes, will clearly be inadequate. Thus building effective coalitions at the local level can have financial as well as political benefits.

Thirdly, black women's organisations which work on issues of violence against women may find potential allies in burgeoning projects concerned with racist violence. There are numerous connections between violence against women, state repression and racist hostility. The fear of racist attack is an additional burden on women considering escape from abusive households; and the high visibility of a house full of black women also lays refuges in primarily white areas open to further violence. Police collusion in cases of domestic violence is mirrored by their frequent failure to acknowledge racist harassment: their unwillingness to prosecute offenders is common to both events. In addition, the failure of the courts to bring about justice in many cases of domestic violence is matched by a paucity of successful prosecutions against perpetrators of racist murders.[10]

Black men and women working together in a primarily Bengali community in East London have created CAPA, a multi-racial organisation which tackles both sexist violence against women and racist violence against men, women and children. The organisation's philosophy, that violence is indivisible and that no elements of violence against black communities can be left unchallenged, is the foundation for solid work with black women's organisations. CAPA is not the only anti-violence project to have developed a commitment to tackling sexism; the Coventry Anti-racial Harassment and Attacks Network, which ceased to function in 1992 due to lack of funds, nevertheless developed strong links with local Asian and African Caribbean women's organisations. Similar projects in Liverpool, Newcastle, Birmingham and other parts of London should provide an opportunity for black women's organisations in these localities to create joint campaigns against all forms of violence.

A final area of potential solidarity is black gay activism. While the nascent 'black men's movement' has not yet developed a rigorous critique of heterosexism and homophobia, black gay men have long been engaged in critical thinking on gender roles. Black gay and lesbian autonomous struggles have been

---

10. A. Mama, *The Hidden Struggle*, London Race and Housing Research Unit, London 1989.

characterised by strong alliances between gays and lesbians within mixed organisations as well as between single gender organisations. As such, these organisations are a model for black men and women working in partnership around a progressive agenda, building on commonalities in the face of different gendered experiences. The effective political alliances which black gays and lesbians have forged indicate that there is an opportunity for collective action on issues such as re-defining black masculinity, making links between patriarchal and homophobic violence, health and HIV. Ultimately, black women's organisations that wish to forge such links will need to challenge their own attitudes and to make theoretical links between homophobia, gendered racism and economic exploitation.

As we look to the past for pointers which will take us into the next century, we need to turn away from romantic visions of a homogeneous black community. Black women's activism, with its refusal to remain silent about awkward 'family secrets', threatens the romanticised picture of the road from Windrush which dominates the BBC version of black British history. It pushes us to ask difficult questions about inequalities and fractures within the black community, and challenges us to look to the margins of the black experience, to those histories which are less vocally celebrated. Viewing the years since Windrush through a womanist lens, we make visible the significant battles which black women have had to wage against silencing, exclusion and sexism within black communities. Even as we acknowledge the impact of this exclusion, we also need to avoid creating a hierarchy of oppression in which black men are always seen as dominant. The complex articulations of racism, class, sexuality and gender prevent us from making such simplistic calculations. The Employment Policy Institute survey is just one reminder of those complexities. Nor can we assume that black male politics will take a monolithic form. Instead, we need to seek out those instances where black men are engaged in building anti-sexist and progressive organisations. Black women have much to gain in seeking coalitions with such organisations; black men in turn have much to learn from the grassroots theorising which informed the resistance struggles of OWAAD, and which continues today in the black women's autonomous organisations which are OWAAD's legacy.

CAMDEN NW1

Superb Georgian terraced house in popular residential street. 3 double bedrooms, 2 bathrooms, reception room, study, dining room, spacious fitted kitchen, magnificent 70ft south facing garden, large roof terrace. Original period features.

£279,950 Freehold

CAMDEN NW1

Double fronted period house on 4 floors close to Regents Park and Primrose Hill. Recently refurbished and providing excellent accommodation. 4/5 bedrooms, shower room, bathroom, 1/2 reception rooms, study, conservatory dining room, magnificent fitted kitchen, sunny garden.

£330,000 Freehold

CAMDEN NW1

A fine 3 storey mid Victorian house set in this quiet residential road near Camden Square. Carefully and sympathetically modernised with the emphasis on bright and spacious living accommodation within attractive period surroundings. 30ft thru reception room, 30ft thru kitchen/dining/living room. 2 bedrooms, bathroom, sep w.c., utility, pretty 35ft garden, gas ch.

£265,000 Freehold

PRIMROSE HILL NW1

Elegant part stucco fronted 4 storey terraced house in the heart of Primrose Hill. Close to Primrose Hill Fields and Village. 4/5 bedrooms, 1/2 reception rooms, in need of modernisation. Many original period features, town garden.

Offers on £305,000 Freehold

Camden Town "Home of Nigerians
1943 – 1945

I cycled from Trinity College Cambridge to Camden Town at weekends to meet the Nigerians

They were eating and making merry. they continued to do so till today except that only a few are left in Camden Town, the single rooms are now beyond means.

Sept 1991

Nigeria-London Connections

Photoessay

Femi Franklin and Lola Young

Lola Young reflects on pages from Femi Franklin's family album.

Femi Franklin's photographs and captions were not constructed with a view to publication but were intended for private, familial contemplation. A keen photographer who chronicled weddings and parties professionally as well as for his own enjoyment, Femi Franklin was part of a small but significant community of Nigerians living in north London from the 1940s onwards. In many albums featuring hundreds of photographs, he gives a fascinating glimpse of the social interaction within the north London Nigerian community, and with Jewish and English friends.

In 1991 Femi Franklin trawled the estate agents' advertisements, looking for pictures of houses in streets with familiar names to illustrate his observations about property, ownership and community. He placed the brightly coloured images, with details of prices and specifications, next to his comments and memories. In the small selection reproduced here, we see how Femi Franklin revisited the photographs from the 1940s and 1950s at the beginning of the recession-hit 1990s, noting how house prices in the area where he had lived had risen enormously over the years. A house similar to one bought for £1000 in the 1950s in Primrose Hill was on sale at £350,000 by 1991: the few people who had been able to buy houses there 50 years ago would have been able to make a substantial profit. For the majority though, buying property was not possible.

ROSSLYN HILL, NW3

An absolutely outstanding second floor flat in magnificent period building. 3 beds. Bathroom. Shower room. Large rec. Kitchen. Balcony. Planning permission to create terrace. Must be Seen. Sole Agents.

£220,000

CAMDEN NW1
Impressive mid terrace Victorian house in need of modernisation and refurbishment. With the benefit of a s/c contained basement flat. Close to tube and shops. Upper Floors comprise: 5 Beds. 2 Shower Rooms. Bathroom. Dining Room. Kitchen. Interconnecting Reception Rooms. s/c flat with Reception Room. Kitchen Area. Bathroom. Gas CH. 50ft SW facing garden.

£245,000

PRIMROSE HILL NW1
Two flats available within this Victorian villa set in an impressive and sought after terrace.
Top Floor Flat: 2 Beds. Reception Room. Fitted Kitchen. Bathroom. Separate WC. Gas CH. 86 year lease. £108,500
1st Floor Flat: Spacious double Bedroom. Reception Room. Recently fitted Kitchen and Bathroom. Ample storage. 119 year lease.
£105,000.

PRIMROSE HILL NW1
A fine early Victorian flat fronted house arranged on 4 floors and in immaculate order throughout. Well presented and offering spacious accommodation, greatly enhanced by the preservation of many period features. 4 Beds. 2 Baths. Kitchen with Aga stove. GCH. Period features. DPC. Double glazing. 30ft patio garden.

£395,000 Freehold

Meeting with In-Laws
    We could have acquired one of the properties at Camden, Primrose or Regent's Park

1952/53

THREE

117

In the first image, the quotation marks around 'Home', and the wry comments, suggest an acknowledgement of both the pleasures and regrets associated with the past fifty years, which anticipate many of the ambivalent sentiments expressed during *Windrush* commemorative events. The second page incorporates photographs of friends taken at a party in the same street as the grand house pictured above them, separated by some forty years. The third (rather formally posed) photograph features his wife, Asake (seated left) and brothers/sisters-in-law. There is the hint of regret in his brief remark about what might have been. In a period of rapid demographic and economic change, what was once a tight-knit group became scattered - across London and Nigeria - engendering, perhaps, some sense of loss.

Amongst the many album pages of advertisements, photographs and handwritten text, there are a few sad stories: disagreements resulting in estrangement, and bereavements. Joyful moments are captured too: a delighted girl showing her ballet shoes, a boy at his bar-mitzvah, and parties. There are intriguing images which make you want to know what the people posing were thinking about: underneath an advertisement for a repossessed house, two white women sit on a sofa, flanked by four Nigerian men, two of whom are their husbands, the women's half-smiles enigmatic and slightly sardonic. Femi Franklin's notes suggest some dispute arose between the husbands and him and he closes the page with the comment 'Alas they both failed to make 50 runs.'

The issue of where 'home' is is explored when commenting on further advertisements for apartments in Hampstead. Femi Franklin suggests the flow between Nigeria and London: 'We got married,' he writes, 'at 155 Fellows Road (see the present price) later moved down the same road Steeles Road on Haverstock Hill making all the roads famous in Nigeria.'

Femi Franklin's chronicling of a period of transformation in his own unique style serves to reinforce the power of images to engage and involve us in private dramas with public interest.

Femi Franklin 1917-1994

With thanks to Mrs Asake Franklin, Frank Franklin and Ola Franklin for permission to use Femi Franklin's images.

The racialisation of space in British cities

David Sibley

David Sibley looks at the ways, both real and imaginary, in which the geographies of the city are racialised.

Spaces of containment

In a photograph by Roger Mayne from a collection which appears to date from the late 1940s or early 1950s some white working-class children look with obvious curiosity on a group of African-Caribbean men in a London street.[1] One of the men turns to the camera but the others walk across the picture, past the children, looking ahead. The street is shabby. The peeling stucco terraces do not bear visible signs of any culture, although other pictures in the collection clearly depict the district as a white working-class neighbourhood, populated by mums in head scarves, children swinging from lampposts and posing groups of teenagers with Brylcreemed hair. The photograph presents the black men in the street in transit, as if they do not belong, but as a source of curiosity rather than the subjects of overt racism.

About forty years later, at a street corner in Chapeltown, Leeds, a CCTV camera on a bulky, dark grey pillar looks down on Cantor's fish and chip shop.

---

1. Z. Cheatle and M. Mack, *The Street Photographs of Roger Mayne*, Zelda Cheatle Press 1993.

This oppressive piece of street furniture is quite out of scale with the Victorian buildings. Its rotating and zooming lens also takes in the chemist's shop and a bus shelter which provided a meeting place for black teenagers pre-CCTV, and, across the street, two Caribbean fast-food shops and a hairdresser's. This surveyed space was formerly the Front Line, a Temporary Autonomous Zone secured by young black men during the 1970s and 1980s but now broken up and dispersed by the control apparatus of the local state. Only the name survives. Front Line Builders are doing a shop conversion further down the road.

Paddington in the 1950s provided a toehold for Caribbean migrants, their presence both resisted and exploited by landlords. Chapeltown in the late 1990s signals containment and surveillance. We have moved from what may have been seen by the dominant white society in the 1950s as a temporary or transient black presence in areas of rented accommodation to a space - black inner city - which has become fixed in the mental maps of control agencies, and institutions like housing associations and building societies. Containment suggests strong and clear boundaries, and this seems to be reflected in some external perceptions of black space. Thus, police actions in the recent past suggest that the northern boundary of black inner city Chapeltown was located about one hundred metres beyond the front line, next to the old Rugby League headquarters. This is where the vans parked before they moved in for a drugs raid. The way in which this space has been defined from the outside suggests an unambiguous geography of threat, a simplification of social space which amounts to a black inner-city stereotype.

'Stereotype' is a term used almost exclusively in relation to people, but it might be fruitful to elaborate on ways in which aspects of the material world could be thought of as constituents of stereotypes. Object relations theorists write about the self and the world splitting into good and bad objects, with the bad self, associated with a fear of a loss of control, being projected onto bad objects, that is, stereotyped representations of others. Conversely, the good self is projected onto objects of desire. Both good and bad are contained in the same stereotypes. However, with one or two notable exceptions, there has been little examination of connections between people and place in psychoanalytical terms.

As a label for a particular kind of space, 'black inner city' combines strong images of good and bad in both people and the built environment. Media representations of inner-city disturbances and uprisings during the 1980s clearly echoed much earlier portrayals of colonised peoples and places. Places like Brixton and Toxteth were represented as disordered landscapes where North American images of competition and survival - given academic respectability through the writing on urban ecology by Robert Park and other Chicago sociologists during the 1920s - were imported by some newspapers to convey the impression of a wild and uncontrollable nature. This characterisation of the inner city as wild and uncontrollable echoed the perception of colonial administrators in Africa or India, but it also signified a more general disorder, and the threat of some 'other' breaching its spatial boundaries. The nature metaphor suggested that the imagined terrain of the inner city was inhabited by an animalised, de-humanised population. Thus, Paul Hoggett notes the symbolic importance of the cockroach in white racist representations of the Bangladeshi population in the east end of London, the cockroach conveying both an abject other, through elision with the radicalised minority, but also one which threatened to invade the secure spaces of the white population.[2] This fear of movement and invasion can be seen in a related case, namely, the demonising of Rodney King before the 1992 Los Angeles uprising. The mobility provided by the car in a city built around the automobile was not supposed to extend to black men who might threaten the white suburbs through their movement, resisting their containment by driving where only whites were supposed to drive. Thus, Rodney King, a black man driving in a white suburb, embodied this threat of invasion.

The imputed associations between people and place that exist in stereotyped representations of the inner city convey a closeness to nature, a distance from civilisation, akin to the lowly placing of black people in hierarchies-of-being employed by Victorian scientists to legitimate the dehumanising effects of colonialism. This has helped to 'other' the inner city, to render it abject - like the bodily residues with which we continually battle, in order to secure the borders of the pure body. A recent manifestation of this was a description by *Le Figaro* (8.11.97) of the racialised spaces of French outer cities as '*banlieues du cauchemar*' (nightmare suburbs). At the same time, urban disorder,

---

2. P. Hoggett, 'A place for experience: a psychoanalytic perspective on boundary, identity and culture', *Environment and Planning D: Society and Space*, 10, 1992.

as it is perceived from the outside and reproduced in selected verbal and visual images by the media, is also exciting for the outsider. Again, primarily North American, black inner-city images - of basketball courts, graffiti and athletic young men - are used, but to advertise trainers and jeans and similar fashion accessories, suggesting freedom and physicality, a desired closeness to nature.

The association between 'black inner city' and disorder clearly depends on parallel associations between white suburbs and order. As Freud noted in *Civilisation and Its Discontents*, 'Order and cleanliness are essentially cultural demands ... the necessity for them for survival is not apparent'.[3] In the British context, a symbolic suburban order might be particularly associated with white cultures, although some black people have certainly bought into the suburban idyll, which is not just about social homogeneity but also material comfort and tranquillity. This suburban stereotype again has colonial echoes. Richard Dyer, writing on film and representation, has suggested that films about white rule in colonial Africa from the 1930s to the 1960s presented an opposition, between a restrained and regulated white colonial society and black mobs: 'Whiteness was associated with order, rationality, rigidity, qualities brought out by contrast with black disorder, irrationality and looseness.'[4] This translates quite readily to racist portrayals of British inner cities with substantial African-Caribbean populations. Racialised white suburban spaces could be characterised in one stereotypical view of the city as ordered, homogeneous and pure, a circle of virtue enclosing inner areas of deviance and disorder.

> 'The English countryside is represented as pure nature, by forgetting its powerlines, quarries and rotting carcases'

In his historical accounts of social relations in the North American city, Richard Sennett has contrasted the 'purified' suburb, the zone of escape for the bourgeoisie (an escape from ethnic and class difference), and the threatening city, populated by people of various ethnicities, but with the common property that they constitute a source of anxiety for the suburban population. He describes the reaction of a middle-class suburban

---

3. S. Freud, *Civilization and Its Discontents*, Hogarth Press 1930, p62.
4. R. Dyer, *The Matter of Images: Essays on representation*, Routledge 1993.

community in Chicago to a spate of robberies in the city in the late 1880s: '...only a state of rigid barriers, enforced by a semi-military state of curfew and surveillance, would permit it to continue to function ... everyone knew what was wrong and what was wrong was overwhelming; it was nothing less than the power of the "foreigner"'.[5] Sennett is suggesting a denial of difference, a displacement of aspects of the bad self onto others through the construction of an imagined geography. Ethnicised, or racialised, fear illustrates the projective and fantastic quality of the construction of ethnic identities. In cases like the one described by Sennett, the feeling of threat depends on the acceptance of a cultural stereotype, a distortion of ethnic difference, and a place stereotype. It requires a simplification of the social geography of the city into a pure suburban zone and a defiled inner city. Suburban factories, sewage farms, DIY centres and racialised minorities are filtered out of the picture to emphasise the virtue and purity of the suburbs; similarly, the English countryside can be represented as 'pure nature', by forgetting the power-lines, the quarries and the rotting carcasses and other unsavoury features of modern farming. By creating a simplified suburban space in their imaginations, people can scurry back home to the ghetto they have created from their fantasised identities.

These geographies are not entirely imaginary, however. Imaginings feed into transformations of the built environment and affect social relations. Suburbs are, in varying degrees, ordered environments, where minor nonconformist acts - for example not mowing the lawn - may be met with disapproval by the neighbours, and the virtues of conformity and order may be used to sell new residential developments. If there is a consensus about the value of spatial and social homogeneity, a collective negative reaction to difference is more likely than in an area of mixed uses and social heterogeneity. Conversely, disinvestment in inner cities and the withdrawal of financial services, practices based on supposedly rational assessments of risk but affected by stereotypical views of inner-city populations, serve to contribute to dereliction and decay. Thus we can see in a city like Leeds a fairly clear line separating

5. Richard Sennett first discussed this in *The Uses of Disorder*, Penguin, 1970. The Chicago study is in R. Sennett, 'Middle-class families and urban violence: the experience of a Chicago community in the nineteenth century', in T. K. Haravan (ed), *Anonymous Americans*, Prentice Hall 1971.

owner-occupied space and an inner-city space, Chapeltown, which is virtually disconnected from the owner-occupied housing market. Chapeltown is a district where houses sell, if at all, for a small fraction of the price of similar property half a mile away in predominantly white suburbs. This racialised inner-city space is characterised by housing association and council tenancies, some derelict properties, and a feeble retail sector, with a marked absence of banks, building societies and large supermarkets. The correspondence between this racialised space and the distribution of African-Caribbean, African and South Asian people in the city is not particularly close, however. The northern suburbs, beyond Chapeltown, for example, have a significant black middle-class presence, but still the imagined black inner city is fixed in space by the decisions and practices of banks, building societies, the city council and the social control agencies. To some extent, the real condition of the built environment then confirms the imagined condition of the inner city.

Marginal spaces, marginalised people

I now want to broaden the discussion of race and space in Britain to consider relationships other than the real and imagined associations between black populations and the city. Ideas about who belongs or does not belong in a place or in a particular district of the city can have a powerful effect on the residential experiences and opportunities of racialised minorities, but the 'space of belonging' assumed in much racist discourse is not solely the inner city.

The simplified view of space embodied in the inner-city/suburb distinction, one which consigns black people to the inner city, has a parallel in the opposition of urban and rural, city and country, with the latter being the home of core English values and the former the source of alien, cosmopolitan values. Thus, city and country are also coded in racial terms, as Ingrid Pollard has illustrated powerfully through her photographs of a black self in a white landscape. These imagined geographies involve encirclement and containment, but British cities have other racialised spaces of exclusion, residual spaces associated particularly with gypsies and others with nomadic traditions. These are less visible spaces, less politically charged than black inner cities.

Gypsy sites in English cities are often unnoticed. They are commonly located in districts which most people avoid, signalling the success of the sedentary society in marginalising the nomad over the last thirty years. One approach to an official council site in Hull, for example, is by a footpath through a semi-derelict industrial area. The path takes you through the weed-strewn remains of an old cement factory and past mounds of gravel to a busy road fronted by a cocoa mill - a marker of colonial exploitation - and a chemical works. Across the road, behind a high wall, is the home of about twenty-five gypsy families, the site itself hemmed in by another chemical plant, an incinerator and a refuse tip. The locale conveys in a tangible way the meaning of 'residual space' and 'space of exclusion': a group of people who were considered to be a polluting presence elsewhere in the city is consigned to an area marked by serious air pollution and the pollution of material residues.

At the entrance to the site, down a side-street cleared of its terraces since the area was declared unsuitable for residential use, is a house trailer which provides a base for the *gaje* (non-gypsy) warden. It is positioned so that its large rear window looks out over 'gypsy space'. But this gypsy space is not shaped by gypsies. It is a sterile, concrete grid filled in with standings for trailers, identical breeze-block buildings with toilets, wash rooms and some storage space, and a patch of ground next to each trailer, some with grass and one or two with the edges softened by flowers and shrubs. This is a disciplining grid on which families have had to modify their social relationships, their modes of interaction and the ways in which they modify their environment in order not to appear discrepant or disruptive, to be marked as trouble. Gypsies are seen to be in need of disciplining because the way they organise their lives, combining work, living space and recreation in the same locale, as all nomads have done from necessity, violates widely accepted ideas about spatial order in the built environment. They do not recognise the separations deemed to be desirable in *gaje* society but their own separations, their strong sense of boundary which keeps apart the pure and defiled, are invisible to those who designed and enforce the site rules. Recently on this site, 'Johnny', a great-grandfather in his seventies, put a shed on his patch of grass. This broke the rules so he was evicted.

Surveillance by the warden and a list of site rules tend to keep the adults indoors. Breaking up cars, sorting scrap metal and lighting fires, activities that provided a focus for collective experience, are strictly prohibited; so most adults concluded that it was better to live on welfare (before welfare- to-work), watch television, socialise inside the trailer or drive off the site to visit relations or go to a pub where their gypsy identity does not result in exclusion or harassment. On the site, the inside of the trailer is all that is left of gypsy space, a space where gypsies decide what is clean and what is polluting. Gypsy sites, like prisons, demonstrate how the state attempts to isolate and then transform a discrepant minority, discrepant in this case because of its ethnicity and nomadic tradition. The concern to regulate the lives of gypsies on sites through the imposition of an unrelieved rectangular grid, and by requiring residents to conform to the separations signalled by the design, is an instance of a 'micro-form' of discipline, which is functional within a larger system. There is an intention to effect cultural change through discipline. Ironically, the stated intention of the architects of the legislation which obliged local authorities to provide sites was to make possible the continuation of a nomadic way of life. Like Australian Aboriginal settlements, which John Pilger has characterised as a form of administered squalor, gypsy sites have a low level of material provision combined with a high level of control. The purpose of sites seems quite transparent, but gypsies are not all subject to the same control regime. Some sites seem highly controlled but others demonstrate the ability of gypsies to transform space so that sites become more like autonomous zones. I doubt that this is conscious resistance. It is more a reflection of differences in the local authorities' enthusiasm for policing sites. They are all racialised spaces, however, encouraging a sedentary life, but one that has to be lived in a degraded environment. Site locations are invariably the outcome of efforts to minimise conflict, or to distance from disgust.

In 1994, the idea that there exists a space of a white, middle-class Englishness, from which nomads are implicitly excluded, was reasserted with the introduction of legislation to secure the countryside for 'the rural community'. The Criminal Justice and Public Order Act of 1994 nowhere mentions gypsies, but in its public order clauses it identifies various transgressive acts - attributed to nomads, hunt saboteurs and other animal rights activists, ravers and festival goers - which were to be criminalised by strengthening laws of trespass. It also repealed the section of the 1968 Caravan Sites Act dealing with sites for travellers, so that those travellers, including gypsies who were not already accommodated on sedentary sites, whether council owned or private, were now liable to be fined or jailed for leading a nomadic life. Implicit in the Act and in earlier parliamentary debates was the idea of a harmonious *English* countryside populated by some imagined rural community from which various youth cultures and nomads were excluded. This notion of people belonging or not belonging in the countryside was encouraged further by the Countryside March in London, in March 1998. This was a demonstration by 'country people', who saw themselves as embodying 'quintessential national virtues', even though they were arguing a case for their cultural distinctiveness, claiming a way of life different from those in the cities.

This idea of a rural community, and an unsullied English landscape representing true Englishness, is connected with imperialist discourse. Imperialism produced alien others who might violate the boundaries of the rural community. They threatened its sanctity and represented a danger to English values. Thus, as James Donald has argued, in Sax Rohmer's *The Mystery of Dr Fu Manchu*, 'ideal rural peace' is seen to be made insecure by Fu Manchu, the stereotypical Oriental other who brings to the English countryside the threat posed by the racialised, colonised peoples of the British Empire.[6] In the face of this imagined threat, it became necessary to emphasise the homogeneity and harmony of rural England. Today, 'the city' as a cosmopolitan space and the home of deviant sub-cultures fulfils the role of the Empire as a source of alien intrusions. The fixing of this rural English space, in which all heterogeneity and difference is suppressed, signals the exclusion of all racialised minorities (and several others).

The geographies of racialised minorities in Britain are complex. Census data, or a bus ride from the outer suburbs of north London or Leeds or Birmingham to the city centre, demonstrate that a spatial category like inner city fails to capture the salient aspects of black or South Asian residential distribution. However, people who are anxious and fearful about racialised difference, and concerned about a loss of power, need simplified mappings; they need to locate imagined threats in particular places. So, 'inner city' becomes another country, a convenient depository for anxieties about mixing and merging, about the breaking down of the boundaries of the self and the group. In turn, 'the city' fulfils the same role when opposed to some tranquil English countryside. These imagined geographies, with their echoes of Empire and colonialism, are to some extent realised, however. Anxieties translate into calculations of risks, surveillance technologies and legislation, which keep people in their place or remove them to the margins.

---

6. J. Donald, 'How English is it? Popular literature and national culture', in E. Carter, J. Donald and J. Squires (eds), *Space and Place: Theories of identity and location*, Lawrence and Wishart 1995.

The hanging baskets of Wood Green

A story

Mike Phillips

Seton grew up in Wood Green. Or, to be more precise, this was where he had lived during the crucial years of his adolescence. When he left his parents' house to go off to university it was a kind of escape, and for years afterwards, whenever things were going badly, he used to congratulate himself with the thought that, at least, he wasn't still stuck in the place where he grew up. In the circumstances, when he eventually bought a house in Wood Green, the move felt like a kind of defeat. It was as if he had tried to make it in the wider world, failed, and been forced to look for refuge in the place where he had his origins.

In a sense this was true. For something like thirty years he had been living, more or less happily, in various different parts of London. Of course, he had avoided spending any time south of the river, and East London was unknown territory. Central London was his magnet, and he thought of Camden Town as a forbidden gateway to the hinterland of North London, a border that he had no desire to cross.

All this changed at the time of his second marriage. Seton owned a small flat near Notting Hill, an address which had become increasingly desirable. His new wife owned a similar flat in South London, and she moved in with him while she tried to sell it. The disadvantages were immediately apparent. The flat, which had been cosy and comfortable for one, seemed cramped and crowded with two people living in it, and when Seton's wife began moving in her clothes, her chest of drawers, her Welsh dresser and her bookshelves, it was clear that they would have to find new accommodation. When Seton's wife started her pregnancy, the matter became even more urgent. 'The child needs a garden to run around in,' she would remark wistfully whenever they discussed the sort of place they were looking for.

The indications were clear. They had to move out of Central London in order to find the sort of house they wanted at a price they could afford, and one day Seton, reluctant, but egged on by his wife's enthusiasm, found himself bidding for a house only two streets away from where his parents had lived.

After the flat their new house seemed surprisingly spacious, full of light and handy, unexpected corners. The garden, too, was a surprise. As a boy Seton had been bored by the whole idea of gardening. Now he came home after work with a feeling of anticipation and went out immediately to pull up the weeds and check the growth of the tiny green shoots which sprouted from the seeds he'd planted. Soon after they moved in he bought several wire baskets and filled them with geraniums. He loved the way that the thick waxy green leaves fell over the side and crawled down the wall, and when he thought of the garden during the day it was the baskets to which his imagination leaped.

Later on it struck him that the pleasure he got from the garden had been a fortunate discovery, because, for a while, walking the distance between his house and the tube station was enough to throw him into a mood of restlessness and depression. To begin with, the High Street looked different. The rows of shops had vanished, to be replaced by a giant shopping mall, but the rest of it was as he remembered, and during the first week he was continually attacked and overwhelmed by a flood of unpleasant memories. Pushing his child's pram along the High Street he kept on noting markers in a teenage landscape of disappointment and insecurity. On this spot he had been stopped and questioned by the police, suppressing his anger while passersby glared disapproval.

Standing at this traffic light he had considered tearing up his school report, anticipating his mother's disappointment and his father's anger. A few yards further down the road, on the corner near the tube station, his sister, eleven years old, had been walking home from school when a man had leaned out of his car and spat on her. 'Go back where you came from,' he shouted.

These events were more than thirty years in the past, but for Seton, it was as if he'd climbed into a time machine, and getting out half an hour later, had found three decades of change had taken place behind his back. This impression was reinforced when he met his neighbours. The family who lived in the house on the right were white people. English. The sort of English people who had lived in the district for several generations. Bert worked as a security guard somewhere in the City. His wife Elly was a dinner lady. Elly's mum was a white-haired presence who lived in a wheelchair and cackled sweetly at the baby when they went past in the street. Sometimes they paused to exchange comments about the weather, blocking the pavement for a moment, the wheelchair tilting as the granny leaned over to look into the pram. The family on Seton's left were as different as chalk from cheese. The mum there was Jean, a sturdy Jamaican woman, with a youthful, bouncy manner, and three grownup sons, the noise of whose electronic rapping and amplified bass thundered through the walls all week, except on Sundays, when the sound would switch to the tremulous cooing of hymns, punctuated by a gabble of argumentative sermonising on the radio.

To Seton both of these families seemed intensely familiar, as if he had known them most of his life. By coincidence, when he had lived all those years ago with his parents, the neighbours had been so similar that they could have been, give or take a few minor differences, the same people. He had been about fifteen then. Moving in, the first thing he had noticed, with the unerring instinct of adolescence, was the fact that the white family on the right, the Greens, had a daughter of the same age. On the second day, across the garden fence, he had made her acquaintance. Seton could no longer remember her name. He remembered, though, her mass of curly brown hair and her eager grin. That was all, because, in spite of his best efforts, her mother, Mrs Green, was a dragon who kept a stern and tireless watch over her daughter, and he could hardly begin speaking to her, in the back garden, or on the pavement in front of their house, before being interrupted by a shrill bellowing from indoors.

'Leave that woman's daughter alone,' his mum said irritably, after this had happened a few times.

There was no point in talking about it, he knew, but it was clear to him that the presence of a black teenager next door had thrown Mrs Green into a frenzy of apprehension, and that, whatever the cost of her vigilance might be, she was determined to resist any further familiarity. Seton had grown accustomed by now to the terror and passion which his mere existence could provoke from some white people. In the circumstances it was clearly hopeless, and he resigned himself to ignoring Mrs Green and Mrs Green's daughter for the duration. The mother at least, he thought, was a dyed-in-the-wool racist whom no appeal would ever shift, and he would probably never have spoken to either of them again, except for the peculiar thing that happened at his sister's wedding.

This was about a year after they'd moved. His parents insisted that the neighbours had to be invited, because they would have to put up with the noise and the coming and going. They won't come, Seton thought, but on the day, they were all there, even Mrs Green and her daughter. The strangest thing about this was that although they had never exchanged more than two words, the Greens smiled at him, moved through the house easily, and seemed to be enjoying themselves. Even stranger was the way Mrs Green behaved towards Duncan. Duncan was a distant cousin who had arrived from the Caribbean at about the same time as Seton and his family. A couple of years older, he was famous for his charm and self confidence. He was already an accomplished musician. He played cricket for the junior team of a county side, and at the time of the wedding he was about to go off to university. Unlike Seton, Duncan never seemed disturbed or inhibited by the hostility or unfriendliness of the white people around him, and everyone who knew him predicted that he would be a great success. Women clustered round Duncan like bees to a honey pot, and to Seton's astonishment, Mrs Green was no exception. In the midst of the crowd she stood by Duncan, chatting to him, smiling and touching him. As he left, Duncan, casually and seemingly without reflection, approached Mrs Green and without hesitation, kissed both mother and daughter on the lips.

Flabbergasted, Seton watched them smiling and blushing and waving Duncan goodbye. On the surface he should have been reassured, but a terrible thought now struck him. Suppose he'd been wrong about Mrs Green, and the truth was that she simply didn't like him. For some reason this was a much more disturbing idea, and he would have preferred to be able to keep on thinking of her as an intractable racist.

Thirty years later Seton could smile when he remembered. Now he was a grown man and a parent himself his perspective on what had been going on in Mrs Green's mind had changed. 'The daughter was a hot little number,' he told his wife. 'And I was a randy little sod with holes in my trousers and lust leaking from every pore.'

Separated from those times by thirty years, he could see himself from the outside, but even so the memory made him determine to keep his distance from the neighbours. On the other hand, he was soon seduced by their friendliness. In Notting Hill where he'd lived previously, the neighbours were polite enough, but most of them were middle-class office workers who decamped for the country at the weekends and holidays and went out for their meals at night. When they met on the stairs or in the street there was nothing to say. In comparison his new neighbours brought presents for the baby, warned him when the dustmen changed their schedule, admired his geraniums and sent Christmas cards.

In less than a few months Seton's feelings about the place were completely altered. Now he walked the High Street without thinking about the past, his eyes scouring the shelves of the shops for packets of seed and other useful things, nothing in mind apart from his baskets of geraniums.

G oing out early one morning for a paper he saw his neighbour, Elly, coming the other way. He was about to smile and make some inane remark about what a bright day it was turning out to be when he noticed that she was crying, her shoulders hunched, and a bunch of tissues clutched in front of her face. He stopped and looked at her with an automatic concern.

'What's wrong Elly?'

She wasn't hurt she told him. She was crying, instead, because of the anger and frustration she felt. She told him the story rapidly. She had been wheeling her mum to the bus she caught every day to the day centre near the Town Hall. As she was about to hoist her on to the platform, a young girl had jostled them more roughly and longer than could be accounted for by accident. 'Do you mind,' Elly said, 'not jostling my mum?' Instead of apologising the girl had rounded on her shouting abuse. As a final touch, as the bus moved off, she had turned, and hawking phlegm up out of her throat, she had spat copiously on Elly.

Even while Seton registered his indignation and sympathy, he knew what she was going to say next.

'Excuse me,' Elly said, a touch of uncertainty in her voice, 'I'm not being funny, but it was a black girl. I don't know why she acted like that. I'm not that way. I've never had no trouble.'

Walking on towards the shops in the spring sunshine Seton thought about the incident. A wheel had come full circle, he didn't know how or why. Back in his garden he pottered around weeding, wondering whether Elly was watching him and what she was feeling. After a while, when he had finished watering the flowers he looked at the dripping baskets and came to a decision. He started to unhook one of the baskets from the wall of the shed, then changed his mind again, picked up the secateurs and snipped a flower from each one. Feeling a little mean he tied the bunch together and walked through the house. Propping the front door ajar, he walked along the pavement to Elly's house, holding the geraniums in front of him like an offering.

The limits of inclusion

Western political theory and immigration

Phil Cole

Phil Cole *argues that the question of who is admitted as a citizen cannot be separated from the question of internal citizenship.*

The arrival of the *Empire Windrush* at Tilbury docks in 1948 is taken to signify the beginning of a story. My concern in this essay is not so much with the accuracy of singling out that beginning; I want to take issue with what the story is understood as being about. The focus of the celebrations surrounding that moment have been not the journey, and not even the arrival, but the problems and challenges that have faced people in their efforts to belong within the United Kingdom. The most important challenge is taken to be the building of a genuinely multicultural community in which people co-exist as equally respected citizens. The issue of citizenship itself is taken to be a question of participation, rather than admittance - an internal question rather than an external one. The problem of who is a member of the political community in the basic legal sense, certainly at the level of political theory, is taken to be settled, and the challenge now is to spell out what that membership entails, in terms of rights and duties and opportunities to participate. And the rhetoric of citizenship at the level of practice, as employed by certain groups in the United Kingdom, is similarly not to lay claim to 'mere' membership, but to a level of active participation in the community.

This particular story is, of course, of central importance, but there is another story that is in danger of being overlooked - the continuing story of mass global migration and its impact on the world political system. The argument of this essay is that the priority accorded to the project of the construction of an inclusive political community, rather than to the question of who can be admitted to that community, renders that project incoherent.

First, while an essential element of the construction of an inclusive community is to confront institutional racism within the nation state, it must be remembered that the most intense form of institutional racism typically takes place at the borders of the state, and that we are writing at a time when western capitalist states are increasingly hardening their borders to protect themselves from what they characterise as a flood of migrants from the poorer parts of the globe. This concern for those still on the outside is not disinterested, as those borders are increasingly policed through internal structures, such as access to welfare, and this can only intensify the institutional racism already in place; in addition, the borders within the European Union, supposedly open to EU citizens, are still highly racialised.[1]

Secondly - and this is the primary concern of this essay - there is a problem at the level of theory, in the turn by radical political movements (such as the women's movement, the physically disabled, as well as black community groups) to the idea of citizenship as the key to an inclusive politics which will be capable of combating their marginalisation. It has to be remembered that the idea of citizenship has its place within a western political philosophy which is fundamentally shaped by the question of exclusive membership; the idea of citizenship, by being the key to inclusion, is also the key to exclusion. In working to construct their theories of radically participatory communities based upon democratic citizenship, these political movements are making the issue of admittance more crucial, and more potentially damaging to their project, as the question of who is allowed to participate in these structures becomes central. This essay examines the tensions within western political theory created by the question of immigration, and the subsequent dangers attached

---

1. Gary Younge also notes the growth of anti-immigration parties throughout Europe, which again creates dangers for members of visible minorities already resident in Europe. See Gary Younge 'Borders of Hate', *The Guardian*, G2 Wednesday 17 June, 1998, pp.2-4.

to the politics of citizenship - that in creating a more *internally* inclusive community, we at the same time create a more *externally* exclusive one. It examines how we can arrive at a political theory that explicitly acknowledges the centrality of the question of admittance, and which points to a political practice that can begin to understand itself as genuinely inclusive.

Political theory and immigration

The mass movement of people across the globe constitutes a major feature of world politics as we move into the new millennium. Whatever the causes of that movement - usually characterised as war, famine, economic hardship, political repression, climate change - the governments of western capitalist states see this 'torrent of people in flight'[2] as a serious threat to their stability. Whether this perception is true or not, it may well be that the scale and nature of this migration calls for a radical re-shaping of both political theory and practice, not just for the sake of economic stability, but for the sake of political, social and economic justice.

This re-shaped political theory has to make sense of the mass movement of people within two contexts. Firstly there is economic globalisation - deregulation of the world economic order, and the relative decline in national autonomy over economic issues. This development is seen as at least one of the factors behind contemporary international migration, as people attempt to follow the flow of wealth to its centres; and yet at the same time those centres - western capitalist nation states - are exerting strict control over immigration. The second context for this new political perspective is that relationships between states and peoples must be understood against what is now a postcolonial world - a world that has been radically shaped by European colonialism, and which is still living through its consequences. Hence, not only does the global migration of peoples call for a re-shaping of the political order, it calls for a re-shaping of political theory itself - because liberal political philosophy, supposedly triumphant over other ideologies, cannot cope with this phenomenon within its own theoretical limits.

The point at which this fatal tension is expressed is at the borders of the liberal nation state, and in the practices of immigration control and naturalisation law.

---

2. The phrase is from M. Teitelbaum and M. Weiner, (eds), *Threatened Peoples, Threatened Borders: World Migration and U.S. Policy*, W.W. Norten and Co., New York and London 1995, p29.

With its universalist commitment to the moral equality of humanity, liberal theory cannot coherently justify these practices of exclusion, which constitute 'outsiders' on grounds any recognisable liberal theory would condemn as arbitrary. And yet at the same time the liberal project depends upon those practices - the existence of a liberal polity made up of free and equal citizens rests upon the existence of outsiders who are refused a share of the goods of the liberal community. Francis Fukuyama says of those states he describes as 'posthistorical' (liberal democracies):

> they have had difficulty formulating any just principle of excluding foreigners that does not seem racist or nationalist, thereby violating those universal principles of right to which they as liberal democracies are committed. All developed democracies have imposed limits on immigration at one time or another, but this has usually been done, so to speak, with a bad conscience.[3]

Liberal political philosophy maintains the appearance of coherence at the level of theory through the strategy of concealment: the vast majority of works in liberal theory do not address the question of national belonging and political membership, and only remain plausible on the assumption that the question has been answered in a way that satisfies liberal principles - but this assumption remains highly questionable.[4] If the question of membership is made explicit, it becomes clear that there is an irresolvable contradiction between liberal theory's apparent universalism and its concealed particularism.

However, any politics that considers itself more radical than liberal political philosophy can take little comfort from the severity of this incoherence, especially as many such politics tend to focus on the concept of citizenship. They may argue that they take the idea of citizenship beyond the liberal conception, and see it as a way of making membership a much more central and participatory experience than that allowed for by the liberal approach. However, it is precisely the question of membership that creates the tension, and as more weight is placed upon radically participatory membership, the tension becomes more painful - especially, of course, for those still outside the borders. And so the problem of borders and who is permitted to

---

3. Francis Fukuyama, *The End of History and the Last Man*, Penguin, Harmondsworth 1992, p278.
4. See Margaret Canovan, *Nationhood and Political Theory*, Edward Elgar, Cheltenham 1996.

cross them remains central to radical left political theory.

Exclusive citizenship

The revival of the concept of citizenship within western political theory has been remarkable, especially within politics that regard themselves as radical. However, citizenship has an internal and external dimension, and the external dimension has been largely overlooked. Internally, the question has been how to ensure that all members of the community can actively be citizens in a meaningful sense, and it has been answered in terms of structures and policies that empower all to be equally active participants. Externally, the question is who will be admitted as a member of the community, and in political philosophy this has been interpreted as being a thin, legalistic issue (in practice, of course, it becomes a very complex legalistic issue, and this is especially case with the United Kingdom's nationality law). The focus of most contemporary political philosophy has therefore been on the first question, of empowerment. Will Kymlicka and Wayne Norman, in an important survey of current work on citizenship, illustrate the point. They make a distinction between citizenship-as-desirable-activity and citizenship-as-legal-status, where the former means that 'the extent and quality of one's citizenship is a function of one's participation', and the latter is 'a full membership' of the community in a purely legal sense. They argue that the two concepts should not be conflated, and that most theorists are concerned with citizenship-as-desirable-activity:

> these authors are generally concerned with the requirements of being a 'good citizen'. But we should expect a theory of the good citizen to be relatively independent of the legal question of what it is to be a citizen, just as a theory of the good person is distinct from the metaphysical (or legal) question of what it is to be a person.[5]

If Kymlicka and Norman are correct, political philosophers can proceed with constructing theories of good citizenship based upon participation, and, with a clear conscience, leave the question of citizenship-as-legal-status for the lawyers

---

5. Will Kymlicka and Wayne Norman, 'Return of the Citizen: a Survey of Recent Work on Citizenship Theory', in *Ethics* 104, January 1994, p253.

- the two questions can be disconnected.

The argument of this essay however is that the two questions are inseparable, and to construct a theory of internal membership without addressing the question of admittance is a fatally flawed project. It can only remain plausible on the assumption that the question of admittance has been settled in a way that is compatible with the principles of equality embodied in the structures of internal membership - but this assumption is highly problematic.

The reality is that, at the level of theory, the institution of citizenship cuts in two directions: first, it makes a distinction between *members* and *outsiders* by drawing a boundary *around* the community; and second, it makes a distinction between *citizens* and *subjects* by drawing a boundary *within* the community. In any liberal polity the internal boundary cuts across the individual, in that all members are *both* subjects and citizens - they are subject to the law, but also sovereign over it by virtue of their democratic citizenship. In the ideal liberal polity, there are none who are purely sovereign (above the law) and none who are purely subject to it. (This, of course, is not to ignore the problem of those considered incapable of participating as citizens by virtue of the lack of rational powers required, such as children; but in the ideal liberal polity, this category is kept minimal.) In an important sense, the citizens/outsiders boundary is a distinction between people - those who are admitted as members and those who are not; while the citizens/subjects boundary is a distinction, not between people, but between *activities* - the public activity of the citizen and the private activity of the subject. Again, in the ideal liberal polity, no members are confined *only* to the private sphere.

The problem comes when we realise that these two distinctions are inextricably entangled: the citizens/outsiders boundary is written into the citizens/subjects boundary, and this is why the question of internal membership cannot be separated from the question of admittance. The point of the citizens/outsiders boundary is to constitute and exclude outsiders - but from what? Not necessarily from the territorial boundaries of the liberal state - it is not important to the liberal state that outsiders are excluded from its geographical space (of course many are excluded in this way but the point is whether this can be justified on liberal grounds). Rather, what is crucial is that outsiders are excluded from *participation* in certain activities. If the citizen is entitled to participate in the most valued activities of the community, then the non-citizen must be excluded from those activities. They are outsiders in this vital sense: they are permitted to enter the private realm of the state, but are excluded from the public realm; they can be subjects of the law, but not sovereigns over it. And so the citizens/ outsiders boundary is as much connected to activity as the citizens/subjects boundary - the border that is policed falls in exactly the same place.

Why should this matter? In fact it raises a number of tensions for the formation of a political community. Firstly, it creates a category of persons who are not recognised by liberal theory, who are purely subject to the law with no sovereignty over it. Where their presence is long-term, in the form of 'guest workers' for example, this is particularly discomforting, especially for the 'guests'. Michael Walzer argues that this arrangement is a clear contradiction of the liberal project and should not be permitted - such people should be granted full citizenship or should not have been allowed to enter the liberal state in the first place.[6] Secondly, it creates potential dangers for certain groups of full members of the political community. As the boundaries between citizens/subjects and citizens/outsiders coincide, the way the external boundary is policed will have an impact on the way the internal boundary is policed. In effect, any group which shares characteristics with those identified as outsiders will themselves be in a vulnerable position. Their membership will be constantly questioned; they will be subjected to forms of surveillance from which other members are free, and their access to the public sphere of citizenship will become hazardous. If the external boundary of the community is policed by criteria based on 'race', however indirectly, then those members who share the criteria will be subjected to racism, from other groups and individuals who refuse to identify with them, and from institutions. The institutional racism is inevitable, as the external boundary is increasingly policed at access points to public goods such as social security and education; and so members of these groups will find it increasingly difficult to gain access to public institutions, as institutions such as those associated with the welfare state are used as a site of immigration control.[7]

The political community can therefore only be confident that its public realm is open to all its members in a inclusive way if it can be equally confident that its external boundary is not closed to others in an exclusive way. This is going to be

---

6. Michael Walzer, *Spheres of Justice: a Defence of Pluralism and Equality*, Martin Robertson, Oxford 1983, pp52-8.
7. See P. Gordon, *Citizenship for Some? Race and Government Policy 1979-1989* Runnymede Trust 1989, pp7-8 and Lister 1990, pp52-6.

especially problematic for those who wish to answer the membership question by appeal to 'national identity'.[8] The policing of the external boundary of the state therefore has profound internal implications, and the problems of immigration and naturalisation cannot be set aside, as Kymlicka and Norman suggest.

A postcolonial perspective

To what extent, then, can we draw on the traditions of western political theory in thinking through these issues? Cornel West raises this challenge when he discusses the new political movements he believes must be developed by African American thinkers and critics if they are to make progress towards greater freedom and democracy. An important issue, he argues, is that this new politics must be built upon 'the rich but deeply flawed Eurocentric traditions'.[9] These traditions include powerful critiques of illegitimate authorities, based upon ideals 'like the dignity of persons (individualism) or the popular accountability of institutions (democracy)' (p6). The expansion of freedom and democracy was at the forefront of these traditions, but there was another aspect of them, based upon brutality, exploitation, and the dehumanisation of others. At the same time as the European nations were setting out their own independence and autonomy according to their vision of the dignity of humanity, they destroyed the independence and autonomy of others in the race for colonies and empire, and excluded those others from the boundaries of humanity itself. It is vitally important, says West, to understand this double nature of the European tradition, because the black diasporan struggle for identity and dignity must take place 'on the ideological, social and cultural terrains of other nonblack people', and this entails 'selective appropriation, incorporation and rearticulation of European ideologies, cultures and institutions alongside an African heritage...' (p16).

A political theory that can be applied to the world shaped by the European tradition therefore needs to take the postcolonial perspective described earlier in this essay, and take into account the way relations between peoples have

8. See David Archard, 'Should Nationalists be Communitarians?', *Journal of Applied Philosophy* Volume 13, Number 2, 1996, pp. 215-220; David Miller, *On Nationality* Clarendon Press, Oxford 1995; Ross Poole, 'On National Identity: a Response to Jonathan Rée', *Radical Philosophy* 62, Autumn 1992, pp.14-19; Yael Tamir, *Liberal Nationalism*, Princeton University Press, Princeton 1993.

9. Cornel West, *Keeping Faith: Philosophy and Race in America*, Routledge, London and New York 1993, p5.

been shaped by the history of colonialism, especially relations of power. A criticism often aimed at liberal political philosophy is that it assumes that the political world consists of ready-made independent and autonomous individuals with equal powers of reason and action. While that accusation is not altogether fair, it may be that there is a similar assumption at the level of political communities - that the political world consists of ready-made independent and autonomous nation states, again with equal powers of reason and action: the central problem of political philosophy has been to ensure that all are empowered to be independent and autonomous members of those states, and the focus has been on the problem of internal equality and social justice. Although some theorists have questioned this assumption, they see the problem as essentially to do with internal unity in the face of cultural diversity. What is not addressed in any depth is how inequality and diversity between states themselves can be made sense of within political philosophy, and how such relations between states impact on relations between members of those states. This is not simply a question of international relations (and I am not ignoring the extent and sophistication of international relations theory within the liberal tradition), or of relations between individual members of different states. Rather, what needs to be addressed is how this international dimension affects relations between members of the *same* state. The relations between members of a particular political community can be importantly shaped by the relationships between that community and others. This is especially true in the context of postcolonialism: we must understand how the internal relations between members of a community have been irrevocably shaped by the history of European colonialism. In the United Kingdom, the political, social and economic situation of certain groups is importantly determined by their historical relationship with former British colonies. Therefore any political theory that attempts to 'do justice' to that situation must take this postcolonial perspective.

The idea of citizenship has to be understood in this context, as it has played a central role in European colonialism in setting the boundary between citizens and others. Bryan Turner observes that citizenship has to be seen in the context of the development of nation states and their colonial subjects.[10] The expansion

---

10. Bryan Turner, *Citizenship and Capitalism: the Debate over Reformism,* Allen and Unwin, London 1986, p47.

of political and social rights at the colonial centre goes alongside the decline of the freedom and autonomy of the colonised. 'National citizenship thus involved a contradictory relationship between principles of inclusion and exclusion' (p47).

The point we have reached, however, is one where colonial history not only shapes the relationships between the 'inside' and the 'outside', but, with the mass migration of peoples, also shapes the internal relationships between members of a political community. Homi Bhabha argues that the crucial moment is the arrival of postcolonial peoples within the territory of the former colonial power - people migrate from the colonial peripheries to the metropolitan centre, and this movement of people must have a profound impact upon how that centre conceives of itself and others. And it *should* therefore have a profound impact upon western political philosophy. Bhabha observes that 'the postcolonial perspective forces us to rethink the profound limitations of a consensual and collusive "liberal" sense of community'.[11]

Conclusion

If we take such a postcolonial perspective, the relation between the internal and the 'constitutive outside' becomes the central question for any political theory, with immigration as the point at which the tensions raised by this question are expressed; as a consequence, the notions of citizenship, national identity and nation state become problematic. One possible response is to shift the focus to something more fluid and flexible, in which it is recognised that communities can be sustained without the rigid boundaries which come with the ideas of 'citizenship' and 'state'. Some writers do conclude that the importance of citizenship attaching itself to nation states is already in decline. For example, David Jacobson comments: 'Under the impact of the transnational movement of people, and its reforming of the way social and political community is constituted, the nation-state is being 'unpacked".[12] The way forward, according to such a view, is first to reconstitute the political community in a way that liberates it from the need for rigid membership practices, and second to increase the scope and power of international,

---

11. Homi Bhabha, 'The Third Space: Interview with Homi Bhabha', in Jonathan Rutherford, (ed), *Identity: Community, Culture, Difference* Lawrence and Wishart, London 1990, p219.
12. David Jacobson, *Rights Across Borders: Immigration and the Decline of Citizenship*, John Hopkins University Press, Baltimore and London 1997, p133.

rather than national, codes of human, rather than citizenship, rights - the emergence of an 'international constitutional order based on human rights' (p136).

Of course, such a global approach has to be seen in the context of the much less benign growth in global capitalism and global inequalities, with the decline in national sovereignty, welcomed by Jacobson and others, paralleling a growth in the power of bodies such as the World Trade Organisation, committed to the protection of free trade not human rights. This aspect of globalisation, has 'major structural implications' both for the former colonies and for the former 'colonizers and dominant geopolitical powers'. However, there is an inevitable attraction to an order in which individuals and groups have their integrity protected by internationally recognised rights, rather than having to depend upon rights conferred by a nation state, which, because of its history, may regard them as alien, dangerous, and unwanted.

This brings us back to the *Windrush* celebrations. Ideally, everybody should celebrate the ways in which post-1948 immigration has shaped British society. However, one possible understanding of these celebrations is that they pick out a particular audience, and that that audience is identified as black, and therefore as essentially connected with immigration despite the fact that many of its members were born in Britain. In order to resist such an understanding, this 'audience' must find a way of celebrating its particular connection with immigration, while resisting the identification of itself as forever immigrant, and therefore as a tolerated presence.

One form of this dilemma is the way we have been repeatedly told that the price for good 'race' relations is strict immigration control, and this argument is used to justify the racist immigration and nationality laws enacted since 1962. The truth is that the hardening of the external borders has brought with it increased internal control and hostility, and that an alternative strategy of greater flexibility of movement might have resulted in recognition of the right to be here, rather than mere tolerance. And so, while we engage in the struggle to build an inclusive political community of equal respect and recognition, we cannot afford to set aside the question of its external boundaries and who can cross them. If we do so, we may find that the radically democratic community we think we have built is in fact a highly exclusive club, and that our membership of it is up for 'democratic' review.

A game of two halves
'English' identity fifty years after Windrush

Bilkis Malek

Bilkis Malek *focuses on the insights football culture gives us into the ambivalences of the English psyche.*

1997 was the fiftieth anniversary of the independence of India and Pakistan. 1998 marks the fiftieth anniversary of the arrival of *Empire Windrush* and the first wave of post-war migrants from the Caribbean. The fact that the commemoration of these historical moments have attained some significance both on television and in the media is evidence that the English have not been able to ignore the presence of the 'margins'.

Perhaps one of the most valuable inclusions in the media's programme of events has been the personal narratives from those first waves of migrants. A number of themes and experiences can be identified across these narratives. One of the most common of these is the hostility of the indigenous population, and the subsequent difficulties in finding housing and employment. And these features convey something about how the relations between the migrants and their 'hosts' were defined, and how the former were positioned in relation to Englishness fifty years ago.

But perhaps the single most important outcome from these initial contacts, which would have profound implications for the future of English identity, was that the construction of the English as a 'superior culture', as a 'superior race', was undermined as never before. As many of the Windrush migrants have recounted, 'We couldn't believe that the English had to sweep the roads; drive the engines; carry the luggage...' and so on. Indeed the transmission of these accounts and self-narratives in the mainstream media is evidence of what Stuart Hall refers to as 'the margins coming into representation'.

It is of course debatable whether there was ever a time when the 'English' lived in a cocoon, physical or imaginary, which enabled them to carry on with their lives unaffected or unchallenged by the 'other'. There is no doubt, however, that this dynamic has accelerated in the opposite direction in the fifty years since *Empire Windrush* docked in an English port. Virtually every individual has had to feel something, or hold some opinion, in response to the 'margins coming into representation'.

The aim of this essay is to examine more closely how, in recent years, the indigenous population have positioned/ (re-)defined themselves in relation to the migrant presence. But before venturing into the complexities of the contemporary 'English psyche'[1], it is necessary to identify the context in which the 'margins' have come to occupy a more visible position within English society. Indeed various fractions of this complex dynamic have been explored in some detail by writers including Stuart Hall, Kevin Robins and Kobena Mercer, amongst others. For the purposes of the discussion here, it is important to set out briefly the main points running across this work.

Modern globalisation processes and the decentering of English identity

Stuart Hall describes the period when 'the image of a stiff upper-lipped white middle class male' was *the* central component of a very narrowly defined and distinctly 'English' national cultural identity which stood for everybody in the British Isles. This of course has always been a problematic construction, as it has concealed the social and cultural differences both within and between the various regions (of Scotland, England, Wales and Ireland) that constitute Great Britain.

---

1. The term 'English psyche' is used to refer to the concurrent themes which link together to form the way in which the government, media and general public perceive and define notions of Englishness.

Yet it was precisely by subsuming differences of class, region, gender, race and so on, that Britain's national identity attained its superiority and exclusivity. And, as Hall points out, it was during Britain's heyday as the 'leading commercial power' that 'the colonised Other was constituted ... through the all-encompassing "English eye"... which assumed authority to place *everybody* else'.[2]

Hall - as do others - argues that the nation state, as a homogeneously constituted self-contained cultural entity, is not able to deliver the kind of societal vision that is now required to compete with the most advanced forms of modern capital. The premise on which such an argument is based is that in order for capital to advance it has had to develop and exploit new, more flexible strategies of accumulation - strategies which are still very much built on the logics of mass production and mass consumption but which are also able to accommodate and penetrate to the individual, strategies and regimes which make it possible to deliver a product or service that is tailor-made to the 'specific' requirements of each consumer.

We are entering into a new phase of globalisation, where global expansion, and the success of capitalist enterprises, is increasingly dependent on the ability to read, respond to and exploit the inner differences and contradictions of what were once considered to be the 'great collective social identities' - class, race, gender, nation and so on.

Most significantly, where national economies have been subject to advanced globalisation processes, it has been necessary for governments to remould the national mood in chime with the march of capital in order that they may continue to enjoy economic success. This means, for example, that the notion of the archetypal English toffee-nosed or stiff upper-lipped white middle-class male has little place in ever expanding global markets driven by consumers effusively differentiated by race, gender and class alliances, all of whom expect polite, efficient and quality services. And this has been a fundamental impetus behind the decline of the nation state, which was very much driven by 'master narratives' and the construction of homogeneous, stable totalities. As a result economic and social relations have become more fragmented and decentered.

Something of a shift away from the 'ideal' of a pure white monocultural

---

2. S. Hall, 'The Local and the Global', in A.D. King (ed), *Culture, Globalisation and the World-System*, Macmillan 1991.

national identity can certainly be identified within British politics. The rhetorically patriotic ambitions of figures like Norman Tebbit are being replaced by more 'politically correct' voices, like that of William Hague, eager to be seen to endorse policies such as multiculturalism, anti-racism and equal opportunities.

These shifting patterns have noticeably filtered down to many aspects of British society, from public service provision in areas such as education and health right through to the private sector, including banks, supermarkets and the premier league. Their effects have been very visible. Gone are the days when landlords and employers openly declared their aversion to filling vacancies with anyone other than the 'white English'. Notices like 'No Blacks Or Irish Need Apply' have been replaced with equal opportunity statements. Many businesses have become more conscious of their ability to boast a multiracial workforce or at the very least setting the appropriate targets to create one. Acts of racial discrimination or incitement to racial hatred, whether in the football ground or the boardroom, can now be subjected to legal proceedings (admittedly with varying degrees of success). And comparable initiatives (though by no means identical) to challenge discrimination against other socially disadvantaged groups, such as women, the disabled and so on, have almost simultaneously reverberated throughout many areas of British life.

These shifts in attitude at a political and organisational level have forced open spaces and opportunities for previously marginalised individuals and groups to be represented at the centre of Britain's political and social spheres. Hall describes this increasingly prominent feature of late modernity as the moment when 'the margins come into representation'.

The purpose of the remainder of this essay is to ask what significance, if any, the 'margins' have had on the way Englishness is now constructed in the popular imagination. How far has contemporary English identity become divorced from its older, more exclusive version?

It is appropriate at this stage to acknowledge the important work already carried out to highlight the deficiencies of multi-cultural and anti-racist policies.[3] Furthermore, these policies and their endorsers cannot simply be positioned as

---

3. See, for example, F. Anthias and N. Yural-Davis, *Racialised Boundaries*, Routledge 1992; P. Gilroy, 'The End of Anti-Racism', in J. Donald and A. Rattansi (eds), 'Race', Culture and Difference, Sage 1992; A. Rattansi, 'Racism, Culture and Education', in Donald, J. and Rattansi, A., *op.cit.*

being in opposition to any efforts to perpetuate the subordinating features which dominated the older forms of economic and cultural power. Indeed, as Hall has pointed out, 'the identity specific forms of marketing ... the voice of infinite pleasurable consumption and ... the voice of the moral majority, the more fundamental and traditional conservative ideas ... are not coming out of different places, they are coming out of the same place' ('The Local and the Global', pp30-2). And my intention here is to signal how such contradictions manifest themselves in the everyday language and imaginations of the indigenous English.

In the rest of this article I want to focus on three key features of modern 'English' identity which link it firmly with its colonial predecessor. Firstly, it remains very much a construction; secondly, it represents and maintains a close affinity with white people; and, thirdly, it retains an ambivalent and exploitative relationship with black people. And I want to sketch out some thoughts about notions of Englishness (with a specific focus on issues of race) which are currently being inflected within the culture *surrounding* English football. (To illustrate the relevance of football culture for understanding English identity more generally, reference will be made to other events that have attained national significance.)

A game of two halves

English football is but one site where the dynamics of advanced globalisation can be seen to be in operation. Both the national team and the premier league now boast more black footballers than ever before. The ever-escalating pursuit of success, and demands for entertaining or 'sexy' football, has resulted in an influx of players from abroad. Indeed the presence of overseas players in some premier league squads has reached a point where the common language spoken on the pitches of Stamford Bridge and Highbury has become as much a talking point as the skills on display. These characteristics signal the changing racial landscape of English football, but they do not reflect how the 'English psyche' has responded to the 'margins coming into representation'. This can be described more clearly through an analysis of the violent behaviour of some English fans during France '98, and the ensuing reaction of the English authorities.

Englishness as a construction

On the eve of England's opening World Cup match a small but now significant group of English fans began to impress their trademark on the French city of

Marseilles. Scenes of fans rampaging through the streets, and confrontations with the local police and opposing Tunisian fans, dominated the prematch publicity. Indeed the behaviour of the 'hooligans' had all the hallmarks of what the 'English' would call a riot, and there was hardly a black person in sight!

'The English authorities sought to detach the "true" English character from that of the hooligan'

The extra security measures (including the early closure of bars and the withdrawal of coverage on the big screen) that were introduced in the towns hosting the succeeding three England matches were in vain. For the script written in Marseilles was predictably replayed in Toulouse, Lens and Saint Etienne.

The actions of the 'hooligans' could perhaps be interpreted as a regression to a former (Victorian) nationalism, in which any opposition to the English football team becomes a potential target for reliving or re-enacting the imperial conquests of the past. Such nationalistic fervour was apparent in the reaction of some English fans towards David Beckham's red card offence. This became a main focus of blame for England's exit from the World Cup, and their failure to win 'revenge' from the Argentinians. The severity of emotions involved culminated in a dummy of Beckham being hung outside a North London pub.

Significantly also, the union jack, and anthems such as 'Rule Britannia', are much more popular amongst English fans than amongst supporters of the other national teams within the British Isles. In fact fans from the other countries of the United Kingdom have not always been reticent about expressing satisfaction in the event of an English defeat, which is indicative of the regional animosities within Britain. It also underlines the inappropriateness of the notion of Englishness as symbolic of Britain.

A more implicit indication of the constructed nature of contemporary 'English' identity can be found in the emphasis placed by the English football authorities on the need for effective segregation procedures to avoid future clashes between rival fans. For this is in direct contradiction with the current trend in domestic politics to project a national identity moulded around the themes of 'tolerance' and 'inclusion'.

Indeed the reaction of the English authorities is perhaps of more significance to this discussion than the behaviour of the hooligans. After all, as the revulsion led by Tony Blair sought to remind us, the violent behaviour was not representative of 'real' English fans, who were by far in the majority. Indeed there was no doubt in the prime minister's mind that the majority of English people would be united in their disgust at the inexcusable violence of a few.

But how far can we consider the mood of the majority as evidence of a shift towards a more inclusive English identity? What are the driving forces behind the efforts to project an Englishness which can live with difference, both within and outside its national borders? Have the hooligans really constructed an identity of their own which bears no affinity with the national mood at large? It is possible to delineate some answers to these questions by comparing the reprisals against the hooligans with contrasting reactions to accusations of violence in other contexts.

The close association with whiteness

The scale of the media coverage accompanying the World Cup meant that the behaviour of the English supporters was open to global attention and scrutiny. And it was clear from both their immediate and more considered responses that the English authorities were suitably embarrassed and sought to detach the 'true' English character from the abusive confrontations that marred all four of England's World Cup matches. Yet when the expressions of revulsion are considered in a broader context a cunning association between Englishness and whiteness can be highlighted.

For example, alongside their condemnations of the English fans, representatives from the government and football association repeatedly reminded us of the need to keep things in perspective: about the small numbers involved; about ticketing problems and the breakdown of segregation; about the intimidation from the opposing fans and so on. Such attention to detail has rarely concerned 'the English' when riotous incidents, no matter how minor, have erupted during demonstrations organised by black people settled here. And virtually every area in England with a high migrant population has ascended to prominence and subsequently become sedimented in the 'English psyche' in the aftermath of confrontations between local residents and the authorities.[4] There have been no concerted media or governmental attempts to point to the

---

4. Toxteth, Handsworth, Brixton, Manningham, Southall, Moss Side and St Pauls, to name a few.

good character of the majority in these areas, nor has there been much mention of the provocations endured by those rioting. This situation has not altered despite the 'margins coming into representation' in a variety of aspects of both English and British life.

The significant point here then is that within its own geographical borders Englishness is still easily dissociated from black people. Consequently, in 'foreign' lands it is only the behaviour of the 'white English' that brings Englishness into disrepute. Thus, the need to distance the thuggish behaviour from the 'genuine English' character became all the more urgent, because it was 'white English' fans, with union jacks imprinted on their faces and bare torsos, that were seen rampaging on the streets of France.

The close association between Englishness and whiteness, and the grave implications this carries for black citizens travelling abroad, can be illustrated more clearly by comparing the respective plights of Krishna Maharaj and Louise Woodward. Both these British citizens have been tried and convicted of murder in the United States. It is difficult to assess to what extent their ultimate destinies have been influenced by the respective reactions 'back home' in England. But there is little doubt of the gulf between the two.

Maharaj, a migrant from Trinidad, attained his self-made millionaire status in the 1970s by importing food from the Caribbean. In 1986 he was charged and convicted of murdering two other businessmen in a Miami hotel and was sentenced to the electric chair. Although last year his death sentence was finally lifted, the evidence amassed by his legal team to prove his innocence has failed to secure a retrial. His predicament has earned limited coverage in Britain, and has featured mainly in the ethnic minority press, such as *Eastern Eye* and a *London Special* programme. Despite pleas from his family and friends, the British authorities have failed to intervene. The campaign for his release has not attracted the almost 'fever pitch' interest shown by the popular press and the public in Louise Woodward's case. Because the Woodward case is fairly recent, there is little need in this article to chart once more the pivotal events leading up to her release.

Leaving aside the complexities and details specific to each case, the response 'at home' could hardly be further apart. The adaptation of the Euro '96 chorus - 'Louise is coming home'- to celebrate the reduction of her conviction from first degree murder to manslaughter was symbolic of the national significance accorded to Woodward. By contrast, the 'free Krishna Maharaj' campaign has failed to even raise sufficient funds to secure the presence of crucial witnesses should there be a retrial. Woodward is now back home with her family looking to do the 'normal' things in life whilst Maharaj is still fighting a life sentence from inside Florida's state prison.

To establish more clearly the relationship I am trying to highlight between Englishness and whiteness - on the basis of my preceding illustration I would not wish to be interpreted as depicting a picture of the indigenous English as wholly unsympathetic towards possible injustices facing fellow black citizens such as Maharaj. Reactions to the fatwa against Salman Rushdie are testimony to that. Nor am I arguing that criminal charges being fought by the white English abroad will always elicit the unquestionable support of 'the nation'. There are no doubt numerous cases that have never captured the national consciousness in the way that the plight of Louise Woodward did. But leaving aside the cross-cutting dynamics that combine to mean that some cases attain more currency in the national imagination than others, each of the cases I've just mentioned would suggest that the extent to which the 'national psyche' is aroused and mobilised is highly dependent on what is seen to be at stake for Englishness. Or, more to the point, what is seen to be at stake for 'white Englishness'.

So, for example, the fatwa against Rushdie was seized as an opportunity to establish the qualities of democracy and freedom of speech as integral characteristics of a superior English culture and to re-infer their absence from the culture of Muslims both in Britain and elsewhere. As such, although the reactions of the English were shrouded in a language of human rights and in support of a migrant, they were essentially concerned with emphasising the 'civilised' culture of 'the English', a quality not embodied in the beliefs and practices of Muslims.

And, as I've argued elsewhere, what clearly emerged from the media and public debates of Louise Woodward's case was the importance of maintaining an 'innocent' notion of white English femininity.[5] By comparison the historical and social context specific to Maharaj's predicament have not yet found a route

---

5. See 'Where have all the women gone? South Asian women come home to the English Seaside in *Bhaji on the Beach*', to be published in a forthcoming collection edited by David Rodgers and Martin Corner, *England at the Millennium*.

into the psychological battleground in which the superior qualities of Englishness are defined and defended.

Another significant point emerging from Woodward's case was that the media and public defence of her was constructed very differently from that of two other highly publicised murder trials - those involving the nurses Deborah Parry and Lucille Mclaughlan. The former became very much a 'damsel in distress' episode, with very limited criticism of the American legal process. By comparison, domestic debates in relation to the two nurses primarily revolved around an 'inferior' Saudi judicial system. This again is suggestive of the reliance of the 'English psyche' on narrow constructions, and its discriminatory associations of notions such as 'whiteness' and 'Islam'.

Relations of ambivalence and exploitation

The third point I'd like to highlight is the ambivalent and exploitative position contemporary 'English' identity occupies in relation to its migrant population. The contradictions embedded in such relations manifest themselves almost every Saturday of the football season, where inside the premiership grounds it is possible to find more black players than ever before on the pitch, but a corresponding decline of black supporters in the stands.[6]

Indeed it is the pursuit of superior status in world football that has been the driving force behind the racially diverse composition of players involved in the English game, both on the national and international stage. But the fans of English teams remain largely white. Their personal desires to witness and celebrate the success of their respective clubs may have impelled them to embrace the likes of Ian Wright and Ruud Gullit, but the notion of 'inclusion' intimated here does not seem to have gone beyond the pitch.

It is also important not to forget that success for 'non-white/non-English' sports men and women has often been achieved amidst a torrent of racial abuse and prejudice from supporters and the media, as well as fellow professionals. It is characteristic of contemporary 'English' culture that it resists as much as it embraces notions of multiculturalism and antiracism. Large sections of the indigenous English occupy a very contradictory space in relation to the

---

6. These contradictions perhaps deepen still further when attention is drawn to the complete absence of Asian footballers from the premiership.

association of multiculturalism with Englishness. This confusion is partly caused by people's very different definitions and interpretations of race and culture. But also, and perhaps more significantly, there are numerous spaces in which English culture (like any other) is defined, contested and revised. And the individual's conviction and personal investment in those spaces will vary in accordance with a plethora of factors, both economic and social.

And what of those supporters whose 'thuggish' behaviour was so out of touch with the 'true' English character. My feeling is that many of them have found their own ways (however tokenistic) of appropriating and embodying an identity which positions itself very contradictorily in relation to the margins. And I don't doubt that a significant number of them will have contributed to the reality of the coded message embedded in the World Cup song, 'Vindaloo' (which incidentally was being chanted amidst the violence in Marseilles) - chicken tikka masala has now replaced fish and chips as the nation's favourite dish.

Conclusion

Few would disagree that the margins have in recent years become much more visible in many aspects of English (and more generally British) life. And this is not just within the context of consumption where, for example, the migrant presence has penetrated to the supermarket shelves. (It is now possible to buy ghee, ackee and cheddar cheese from one outlet rather than three.) The 'margins' have also made significant inroads into the business, creative and popular entertainment sectors. Joe Bloggs (Shami Ahmed's business empire), Linford Christie, Hanif Kureishi, Jazzi B, Naomi Campbell and Lenny Henry are household names that are arguably as recognisable as Laura Ashley, Sally Gunnell, Fay Weldon, Robbie Williams, Kate Moss and Ben Elton.

However, contemporary 'English' identity cannot be confined to a particular set of values that are consistent with *either* a rejection of *or* an acceptance of black people as equal citizens. Indeed, the dominant response to the 'margins' is highly contradictory. What can be ascertained with some degree of certainty is that, whatever the response to the 'margins', it is overwhelmingly driven by the pursuit of economic and social prestige for 'the nation'. And this is not just in relation to issues of race.

It is precisely such a contradictory identity that allows Tony Blair to denounce the acts of violence instigated by English supporters during the 1998 World

Cup finals but not to have felt compelled to do the same a year earlier when the English midfield player Paul Gascoigne assaulted his wife. In fact, with regard to the World Cup hooliganism, Blair went as far as calling on employers to sack any employee convicted by the French courts. But then the behaviour of the hooligans was potentially hazardous to England's bid to stage the 2006 World Cup. By comparison, at the time Gascoigne assaulted his now estranged wife, he was still considered a key player for England's chances of qualifying for the finals in France. To have called for Gascoigne to be axed from the national team would probably have been regarded as endangering the nation's place on football's biggest and most prestigious stage.

In his examination of modern globalisation processes, Hall asks the question, 'Is this simply the final triumph, the closure of history by the West ... where it now gets hold of everybody, of everything, where there is no difference which it cannot contain, no otherness it cannot speak, no marginality which it cannot take pleasure out of?' ('The local and the global', p33). Hall goes on to warn that we shouldn't fall into the tempting position of conceding that 'I can't see around the edge of it so history must have just ended'.

The question then becomes one of identifying what promise modern globalisation processes hold for overcoming the persisting imbalances of power and opportunity. This question becomes all the more pressing if the contradictions of contemporary 'English' identity that have been highlighted here are, as Hall suggests, a direct outcome of advanced globalisation.

It is not possible to even intimate the future course that globalisation will take on the basis of a limited discussion of 'English' identity such as the one above. But as a process that has forced open spaces for the voices of the 'margins' to be represented in some of the most exclusive of places, as for example the House of Lords, its positive capacities cannot be underestimated. Unfortunately, the opening up of these spaces is still largely driven by a desire for economic power and social prestige, with any positive outcomes for previously colonised groups being of secondary importance. The reversal of this trend is therefore crucial to any effective and permanent decentering of 'English' identity - or indeed of 'the West'.

Until that moment, the most crippling consequences of that most brutal of cultural identities, which made colonial domination possible, will always be allowed to flourish, and find their own spaces for expression.

Negotiated belongings

The following is an edited version of an interview by Gail Lewis with her twelve-year-old nephew, Simon Hamilton-Clarke. The interview took place in August 1998, about one month before Simon was to start attending secondary school. It was after the BBC four-part television series on the Windrush had been broadcast, but Simon had only seen two of the series when the bulk of the interview occurred. He watched the final two parts about two-thirds of the way through the discussions. Many of the questions grew out of the issues and questions that had been raised for Simon by that series. The questions from Gail appear in italics.

'Necessary bread' - the importance of the Windrush story

Let's just start with what you think the Windrush means to you.

Windrush was a boat which took black people from Jamaica to England, and I think it's really important to me because it's about the history of black people, and I think that history of black people is important ... you don't learn much about it at school - you don't really get to know about it - but it's interesting. If we could just only get to know about black history ... we could learn about our culture, what it's like in the West Indies, instead of knowing only about what is happening around England.

And so is it only for black children that it's important to learn that...?

No, I think it would be important for white people to learn it too ... because some white people have a fairly stereotypical view of black people, and if they don't learn about black people, then they're going to take in the stereotypical views, and think that that's right, and then it's going to carry on from generation to generation.

Give me an example of the kind of stereotypical view that some white people have of black people.

Well, some white people think that black people aren't ... are more athletic than intelligent.

And you think that learning some of the history would help to get rid of that view?

Yeah.

Friends, family and Englishness

If you think of your friends at school, what ethnic groups do they come from?

Well, most of them come from England, but other people come from places like Asia ... and one or two people come from Africa ... and one person comes from Monserratt...

So would you think that learning about all those people's histories would be important? When you talk about black history, do you include other people, not just Caribbean people?

Well I'd include Asian people as well as black people.

And when you say English people, who do you mean by English people, who would you include in that category of English?

Well I'd include white people more ... But I know there are black English people just like me ... a person that's been born in England but their mum and dad - or just their dad - has come from Jamaica or West Indies or somewhere, or India or somewhere like that.

So where do your mum and dad come from?

Well my mum comes from England, and my dad comes from Barbados. My mum is mixed race - her dad was black and her mum was white. Her mum came from England and her dad came from Jamaica. And my dad is black, and comes from Barbados.

So if you had to describe yourself how would you describe yourself?

Well, I see part of me is white and part of me is black.

But if you were at school what would you say ... what nationality would you give yourself?

English.

English, okay, would you call yourself black English then?

Yeah.

And what about, say, your friend Bhavesh - tell me about his background.

Well, he comes from Kenya, but he moved over to England, and now they live here, but he is ... he's Kenyan.

And would you call him black English or Asian English?

Asian English ... because I think that he's more ... because you call Asian people Asian, black people black, I would probably call him an Asian English.

And where would his Englishness come from?

Well, from living here ... and he's been to school here and things...

And what about your dad?

Photo: Lorraine
Hamilton-Clarke

Well yeah, I think he's got a bit of English because he's been here for quite a long time.

Tell us about some other members of your family, who else have you got in your family?

Well, my sister and brother and stuff, they were born in England, and they're black like me ... and everyone else was ... except my aunt Liliane ...
Tell me about Liliane.

I think she comes from Lebanon ... And she came to England like my dad did.

Yep, so what would you call her - you've called your dad Bajan, and you call him black, and you call all of us English but we're all black or mixed race ... what ethnic group would you say Liliane belongs to?

I think she'd be black too ... but more like Asian kind of black.

Tell me a little bit about what the difference might be between our kind of black and Liliane's and Bhavesh's.

Well, ours is African … Caribbean, things like that … and I think Liliane is Arab.

So your family is quite mixed then really isn't it … What's your feelings about having a mixed family like that?

I find it normal.

Windrush **connections/ European exclusions**

And, given all the mix in your family, what connection do you think that's got to Windrush *coming in 1948?*

Well probably if I went back … I'm not sure, but maybe some of my family might have come over on the *Windrush* - like my dad did a bit later on, which I find partly a connection to the *Windrush* … people coming over. I find that a connection to the *Windrush*, because they've come afterwards, but it's basically the same kind of thing … They've come over to England and they were shocked at what it was like in, in the same way as they were before … My dad said that he thought everywhere would be big houses, and that people would be very posh, but when he came over he was surprised, like they were on the *Windrush*, because not everybody was rich, there were poor people, and they weren't very posh.

Say, for example, if you go on holiday to Portugal or Spain or France, and you see people who you think of as black, do you feel connected to them at all?

In a way, because they're like … when we go to France … you see more black people in France, so then you know … you know there's going to be black people there next time you go. But if you go to Spain, there are quite a lot of white people and not many black people, so when you see some you think 'oh there are black people here', and then you feel connected, because you feel a bit alienated being by yourself and hardly seeing any black people around.

And why would you feel alienated do you think? What is it that makes you feel alienated?

Well, you feel that there's more white people around you, and then you wonder about if they're going to be racist or not ... like calling you racist names. Like we got called in Spain, we got called *negres*, which I think is black, but they ... the way they said it, the way they looked at us, me and my family think that they were being racist towards us ... because of the way ... the tone of voice was ... more stressed and ... the way he was looking at us.

Refusing racist exclusions

And when you watched the Windrush *programmes did you learn anything about racism?*

Yeah. I learnt how racist, basically, everybody was, like ... people in politics, politicians like ... Moseley and Enoch Powell - they were very open about racism towards black people, and in Enoch Powell's Rivers of Blood speech, he wanted black people to go back to the Caribbean or wherever they came from... well, I don't think they should. If they're comfortable in England and they want to be in England, then they should be able to stay.

And what about you? I mean, if somebody came up to you and said 'oh you've got to go back', would that have any meaning to you? Would you think there was somewhere 'back' you could go to? I mean, where do you come from?

Well ... go back, I'd say I wouldn't ... agree with that ... Because there are loads of different places that I could go back to, go back to where I came from - like I could go back to Lebanon or the West Indies or I could just stay here ... 'cause I was born here.

From what you saw on the Windrush *programmes, do you think that all white people were racist?*

No.

You're shaking your head very strongly there.

No. Because there was one person who got shot by a teddy boy [GL - *you're talking about Kelso Cochrane*] - yeah … and there were white people that walked through the town at his death. There were black people as well, mainly black people, but there were some white people who went on the march too.

Racism now and then

And what about nowadays, what's it like in school for example, is there racism in school at all?

Not … no … Not so far, no I haven't come across racism.

Oh that's good … and what do you think would be examples of racism if you had faced it?

Well, first of all, name calling, or people touching my hair and saying 'oh your hair is bouncy' and stuff, or something like that - I call that racism too.

Earlier you were talking about one of the stereotypes that some white people have of black people - that they're not very intelligent but they're very good at sports - You haven't had any of that at school?

I think I have … in year 4, I got it from a teacher … well it was not very distinct … I couldn't really tell, but, she was, like, congratulating me more on my physical education things that I did well, and less on the more important things like English and Maths and stuff … but, that was just in one year.

Oh good, that's good. Simon, I wanted to ask you a little bit about the picture that you gathered from watching the television programmes. How is it different from what you know now, from your own life - what is the difference between the late 1940s and 1950s and even 1960s, compared to now, the 1990s? Do you think it's changed at all?

Yeah, I think it's changed a lot … like people aren't really allowed to be racist out loud now, for instance on the TV ... and in the streets too, you don't get people coming up to you and saying 'go back to your country' or touching your hair and trying to make your skin rub off ... You do get, sometimes, stereotypes, sometimes in hidden ways ... like on the news, my mum and dad can hear it -when they're going on about how black people are wrong and stuff like that.... And that black boy who died ... Stephen Lawrence ... the police hardly take his case seriously, and me and my mum and dad think that's because he's black, and I reckon if Stephen Lawrence, say, killed a white person, they probably would have followed it up a long time ago.

So there are some things then that are still around.

Yeah.

But there's changes as well.

Yeah ... Things like giving a contribution ... like news readers ... like Trevor MacDonald and Simon Green, I think they contribute to things.

Going back to what you were saying about stereotyping - about black people being thought of as good at sports but not other things - what does that make you think about the contribution that black sports people have made, like Linford Christie, say, or Ian Wright, or John Barnes, or Andy Cole or whatever? Do you think that's important?

Yeah, I think it's important, because there's quite a bit of racism in football, especially at matches ... You hear constantly in the news about how people are making racist remarks. And in one case, a footballer did the Nazi salute to a white person, to a white Jewish person, on the pitch. And he got banned from football for a long time. I don't think he's come back.

Now that's interesting, what you've said there, because you've talked about racism against a particular kind of white person, a Jewish person - so do you think that some white people can face racism? – it's not just a question of being racists, they can face it to?

Yeah, I think they can ... I reckon Jewish ... and some white people can be Muslim as well.

refusing - again

That's true, that's a good point. But let's go back to that thing about sports, because I'm trying to understand what you're saying about sport: on the one hand you said 'well there's this stereotype, that that's all that we can do', but on the other hand you said 'it's important that we're in football or athletics' or something . So how do you balance those two things up? If people are successful in sports, isn't that just feeding the stereotype?

Well not really, because if there weren't any black people in sports, and if a black person wanted to join in sport, the racism would be very high and they probably, most likely, wouldn't be able to get in for a pretty long time. I'm not saying that black people shouldn't do sports if they want to. I'm saying don't let white people say that you can't be a doctor or somebody clever, just go, do what your heart tells you really.

So do you think that the presence of black people in sport has affected the way in which people might respond to a question about what the population looks like? If, for instance, in 1948 when Windrush came a news reporting team went out and asked anybody in the street what they thought the population of England looked like, what do you think they would have said?

Um, probably white people.

And if they went out in the street now, in 1998, what do you think they'd say?

Well, I reckon they'd probably say a mixture of white people, black people and Asian people too.

Colour, boys, connection

So Simon, if I was to ask you what it's like to be a black boy of 12, what would you say? What are your experiences like?

Well, I have been called racist remarks, but so far it's been fine really.

Right. And do you think it's different from being someone like your friend Joe for example? Do you think his experiences are different because of different colour skin?

Um, probably ... Well I'm sure that he probably hasn't been called a racist remark.

Do you think you've shared things in common though as well?

Yeah ... me and Joe, we like the same music, we talk about the same things, like clothes and ... we kind of think about the same things too ... like ... well, like Adidas and Ben Sherman make of shirts, and Armani jeans ... and on his computer, on e-mail, or on the internet, every time we went to think about something to say ... it would basically be the same thing.

So really then, in that sense, colour didn't matter?

No.

The future

Simon, what do you think about the future? Because you've said that in 1948 it was much worse for black people than it is in 1998, and that although there is racism about now it's not quite as bad. What would you hope it to be like, say, when you're 20?

20!!

In eight years time.

Well, I'm hoping that there would be a lot less stereotypes and ... a lot less racist people too. Especially in films. Basically, black people are always gangsters, or they're policemen, and they always fight against people. And in futuristic films, you always find that it's basically black people that always do the athletic-like movements... Say there was a film, even in comedy, about a professor, it's hardly ever a black person – it *has* happened but it's hardly ever taken seriously, that there's been a clever black person ... That would be good ... instead of having to beat somebody up, not be clever...

Caribbean imaginings ...

One of the things that I meant to ask you about was Barbados. When you were about eight or nine, you had a time when it seemed as though you were talking about and thinking about Barbados quite a lot. It seemed like a place that was on your mind. I was wondering if you could say anything about what you imagine it to be like when you think about it?

Well, I imagine it to be sunny. I imagine there to be a beach and ... I can imagine dad's house, and the church that he went to.

Where do you get the idea about the sun and the beach from?

Well, mainly from the news and travel brochures ... in school we were asked about the rain in the Caribbean - it wasn't Barbados it was St Lucia - and there was a question 'do you think it rains more in St Lucia or in England' and everybody in the class said 'England' but it actually rains more in St Lucia.

If you've done stuff in school about how there is more rain in St Lucia, which isn't terribly far from Barbados, why is it that you think about Barbados as being full of sun and sand?
Because of what I heard ... like some from dad, some of it from the news... and travel brochures.

And how do you imagine your dad's house then? You said you could imagine your dad's house.

Well I think it would be a detached house, fairly nice on the outside ... parts of the house were wooden too, and some were made out of brick ... and the church ... would be wooden ... wooden, white, and with the sign of a cross on top of it...

Would you want to go to Barbados?

Yeah, very much ... because dad tells a lot of stories about all the good things that he's done there, and I'd just like to go.

... and returning (to the discomforts of) home

If you went there, would you say 'oh, I'm going home to Barbados'?

Probably not, I don't think so.

So if you talk about home, where do you mean?

My home here ... in England.

In the third part of the film, some of the young men were talking about how it was very hard for them, as young people in the 1970s and 1980s, to think about the idea of being black and British, or black and English – we've talked about that a bit. What do you think about that idea that they felt ... that they couldn't be black and English?

It was because of the racism around, and because the more important white people didn't really care about them.

But do you think that's a good feeling to have, that you can't be black and British?

Back then I probably would have thought it ... But now that it's not so racist I don't really think ... I don't really think about that ... I don't really think about the racism, so when I think about it, that doesn't really come into mind.

So you don't think it's completely contradictory to say black and British, now they can absolutely go together you think?

Yeah. But part of me is West Indian.
Right, so you would say you're part West Indian, and saying that you're part West Indian doesn't contradict saying that you're black British or black English?

Yeah, it does.
So how do you reconcile, how do you put those two things together?

Just say that I was born in England but my dad comes from Barbados and my grandad comes from Jamaica too. So then it's like I'm partly West Indian as well as English.

When we first started the tape you talked about how you call yourself black English. Do you think you've been influenced at all by watching the video?

No ... but sometimes I think about whether I really should consider black English ... because, after all that they put black people through, why should I say now that I'm partly English as well as West Indian?

I understand what you mean, and it seems as though you're a little bit sad, you sound a little bit sad now. Is that right or am I imagining it?

I am, yeah. It's because of the way that they treated black people.

But do you think maybe, precisely because some people didn't want black people to call themselves black British, that's why we should do that - maybe we should say 'well we're not going to let them tell us who we can be'. Maybe we'll say 'yeah that's who I am and I've got every right to be that'.

Yeah, I think so ...

Hair

Photo Essay by Sonia Boyce

Claire and Afro

Stuart and Afro

All in the same boat?

Roshi Naidoo

Roshi Naidoo looks at cultural texts of migration and argues that while a diversity of experience must be acknowledged the power of collective narratives should not be underestimated.

The arrival of the *Empire Windrush* symbolises the moment when Britain was transformed into a 'multiracial' country, and therefore has come to represent all migrations from Britain's former colonies to the 'mother country'. For some, the conflation of this moment as representing Caribbean, African and Asian migrations in general will echo the ways in which immigrants and their descendants have historically been homogenised by the British state as an undifferentiated mass of intruders - 'coloureds' who threaten the social and cultural cohesion of this green and pleasant land. It could be argued that *Windrush* as the signifier of migration obscures the specific histories of different groups, and erases the centuries old presence of the non white 'other' in this country.

For others though, *Windrush* as a general marker of these historical events allows us to reflect on the strikingly similar histories of migration and settlement different communities share, irrespective of whether they are directly connected to this moment. It represents how seemingly disparate groups have remade that collective label of 'immigrant' to deploy radical, inclusive and politicised identities to fight for justice and equality on these islands. The *Windrush* anniversary also invites us to assess the impact that those of Caribbean, African and Asian descent have had on the shaping of British national identity in the post-war years.

Should the *Windrush* celebrations be embraced or challenged as the symbol of the many diasporas which have reshaped Britain? If we reject the generalised interpretation of its significance then we have to decide who *Windrush* 'belongs' to - all Caribbean people, African Caribbean people, those of Jamaican descent, or maybe only those directly related to the handful of people who docked at Tilbury fifty years ago. To narrow down these categories too far is to lose the significance of the moment as representative of a collective history, but at the same time the problem of essentialising 'the immigrant story' remains real. Is it possible to read the *Windrush* celebrations as having meaning for a diverse audience of Caribbean, African and Asian peoples, while also acknowledging difference, and the distinctiveness of the particular experiences of these groups?

I want to suggest the possibility of such a reading as one of many which can exist alongside other more specific interpretations of what this anniversary means. The autobiographical accounts emerging from the *Windrush* celebrations clearly have a resonance for a wider audience because they emerge from a history of migration and settlement in Britain which many share. The sameness and difference of these stories can be read in the cultural texts which different settlers and their descendants have produced. With this in mind I want to read this collective history against the body of literature in Britain which has charted those experiences, and given shape and form to the complex subjectivities of those born and/or brought up in this country, yet who are tagged with the label of 'second or third generation immigrants'. The remembering and constitution of a collective history via cultural texts also involves the recognition of the ways in which class, gender, sexuality, region, ability, or language, shape those experiences in particular ways. I will conclude by asking what is at stake in the suggestion that we, as Caribbean, Asian and African people in Britain, are all, so to speak, 'in the same boat'.

It seems appropriate that the *Windrush* anniversary should once again produce ambiguous and ambivalent feelings about where the boundaries of cultural identities and political communities be drawn. On the one hand Caribbean, African and Asian communities have consistently challenged regressive homogenised identities; on the other, they have acknowledged the collective identities which have grown out of a shared history. The writer George Lamming noted, in his work *The Pleasures of Exile*, first published in 1960:

No Barbadian, no Trinidadian, no St Lucian, no islander from the West Indies sees himself as a West Indian until he encounters another islander in foreign territory. It was only when the Barbadian childhood corresponded with the Grenadian or the Guianese childhood in important details of folk-lore, that the wider identification was arrived at. In this sense, most West Indians of my generation were born in England.

Lamming's point not only captures how the parameters of community identification can change, but also how coming to Britain has produced particular ways of naming. As Stuart Hall notes, cultural identity, 'is a matter of "becoming" as well as of "being". It belongs to the future as much as to the past. It is not something which already exists, transcending place, time, history and culture.'[1]

Both Lamming and Hall alert us to the ways in which current labels which demarcate the borders of belonging are also in a process of flux, as there are constant negotiations about their limits and inclusions. 'Immigrant' communities are usually characterised as being made up of African, African Caribbean and Asian, but these can be unsatisfying categories. Where, for example, do Caribbean Asians place themselves in this tertiary arrangement? How much is the notion of Africa as a single entity tied up with colonial narratives about the 'dark continent'? Is there too much slippage between 'Asian' and 'Indian'? Importantly, there are continued challenges to the notion that these categories are internally homogeneous. Feminist, lesbian and gay activists, critics and cultural practitioners have rejected the idea that there is, for example, a homogeneous African Caribbean community unmarked by gender, sexuality and other differences. In resisting the idea that political priorities should be defined by heterosexual men they have often faced the accusation that they are compromising black political 'unity'. It is true that to assert the complexities of subject positions is to highlight antagonisms existing between people. However such antagonisms, rather than being divisive, have emerged as useful critiques of the complex operations of power in people's lives, and have shown why it is impossible to decide whether 'race' is more 'important' than issues of gender, sexuality, social class or ability.

---

1. Stuart Hall, 'Cultural Identity and Diaspora', in Jonathan Rutherford (ed.), *Identity - Community, Culture, Difference*, Lawrence and Wishart, London 1990, p225.

Cultural texts are unique places, where the different boundaries of belonging and competing subjective voices can be mapped. Like the subjectivities of those who write them, this body of literature can shift categories of location; the context of diaspora means literature produced in Britain by those of Caribbean, African and Asian descent can be placed in many different literary traditions. For example, a text such as Meera Syal's *Anita and Me* can be read as Asian women's diaspora writing, as Indian writing, British Asian writing, contemporary British writing, British women's writing, or alongside texts by other British based Caribbean, African and Asian writers. This is not a matter of whim, as each context brings particular political significance. Can Caribbean, Asian and African literature in Britain be read together in a way which is politically constructive?

The history of migration to Britain is one which involves culturally diverse peoples, from all parts of the globe, arriving on these shores at different times and for different reasons. Their reception and treatment has been determined by the economic, political and social events, and ideological shifts, of particular moments. Therefore to do justice to the writings which have emerged from these histories it is important to address the specifics rather than to see all 'immigrant' writing as essentially the same. At the same time these specific histories mesh together to create a more general picture of the similar problems encountered by those who came from Africa, Asia and the Caribbean to make their homes in Britain. This is a history of racism, of heavy policing and of discrimination in every area of life. It is also, in part, a history of cultural partnerships and political alliances between different groups of settlers, as well as with white Britons. If the history of 'immigrant' experience can be understood as both particular and general, then 'immigrant' literature too can be understood in these terms.

Post-war migration brought with it an accompanying literature by black settlers, which spoke of the emotional, social and psychological effects of those geographical movements. Although the fictions produced must be read as works of imagination rather than as sociological documents, they are inevitably framed by the historical circumstances in which these writers found themselves. As a result various leading themes emerged as writers attempted to voice the feelings of a generation. Concerns over the location of 'home' reflected the duality people felt of missing the familiarity of their lands of birth, while also acknowledging that as time passed they became excluded from that home in important ways. The hostility faced in the 'mother land' made making an alternative home here full of obstacles, and places left behind often became distant vistas to be viewed through rose-tinted glasses.

The early novels which told of migrant experiences can be read against these issues of economic uncertainty and cultural displacement. Samuel Selvon's *The Lonely Londoners*, first published in 1956, captures one aspect of this, painting a picture of the world inhabited by a group of single men from the Caribbean. Selvon's novel traces the cycle of working, hustling and chasing women which the characters engage in, as their collective dream of one day returning to their respective islands as rich and successful men fades slowly in the face of the realities of life in Britain. For Moses Aloetta and the other characters though, London is not only the harsh landscape where the promises of the 'mother land' collide with the reality of racism, but also a place filled with the romance of locations dreamed of in their colonial education. Galahad in particular is seduced by the city and the promises it has to offer: 'He had a way, whenever he talking with the boys, he using the names of the places like they mean big romance, as if to say "I was in Oxford Street" have more prestige than if he just say "I was up the road"' (pp 83-84).

Selvon's evocation of the legacies of a British colonial education would have had much to say to a wide range of people who, though brought up in places as far away from each other as Durban, Kingston or Bombay, had been raised on the same diet of 'English' literature, history and culture. Coming to Britain was a journey to a land both strange and familiar, and one where the colonial narrative of Britishness jarred with what was encountered here. The oral histories of people from a variety of backgrounds recall how shocking it was to confront white, urban working-class people, when colonial fictions had established Britain as quintessentially upper middle-class in nature. These sorts of shared experiences acted as a reminder that the legacies of colonialism had already established connections between peoples from different parts of the globe, which being in Britain would crystallise.

It should be possible to read a novel such as this alongside other narratives of coming to Britain, without holding it up as definitive. As Susheila Nasta points out, 'few women writers were published at this time, largely because the first wave of immigration to Britain was predominantly male'.[2] Women's writing which emerged subsequently is therefore extremely important in representing other versions of that journey. Feminist readings of migration literature across the boundaries of supposedly homogeneous cultural communities show how similarities of experiences can be mapped without succumbing to the idea that they are the same. For example, there is a body of autobiographical work which tells intimate stories of what migration to Britain entailed for women. Beryl Gilroy's *Black Teacher* exposes the juncture of racism and sexism she met as a young teacher from the Caribbean attempting to build a career in the British

'It is important that migration narratives are read as both particular and general'

education system at a time when black teachers were a novelty. Buchi Emecheta's semi-autobiographical novels; such as *Second-Class Citizen*, tell of the trials of Adah from Nigeria, whose experience of working-class bedsit life contains the added responsibilities of raising children, something not usually incumbent upon male migrants. Sharan-Jeet Shan's work *In My Own Name* is a deeply personal account of a life where migration produces complex feelings about home, and explores the impact of domestic strife on women isolated from networks of support in a new environment.

These writings echo the crossings that people have made across history and geography, and reflect the ways in which subjectivity and cultural identity are caught up in these historical and geographical movements. This raises specific issues for criticism, and reminds us that these texts cannot simply be read as writing which makes 'visible' the 'hidden' experiences of migration. Women's writing and works by those from different cultural communities have provided a quilt of narratives which tell related but distinct tales of coming to Britain, and therefore expose how 'race', gender, culture, language and class inscribe those experiences. However, the themes of homelands, displacement and the locating of the emotional costs of migration can be traced in novels by writers from divergent cultural communities (Jewish, Irish, Greek, etc) and by male and female writers. Therefore it is important

---

2. Susheila Nasta, 'Setting Up Home in a City of Words: Sam Selvon's London Novels', in A. Robert Lee (ed.), *Other Britain, Other British - Contemporary Multicultural Fiction*, Pluto Press, London and East Haven 1995 .

that migration narratives be read as both particular and general.

It is not just at the point of post-war migration and settlement that I want to pursue this theme. For the writers of subsequent generations, issues of homelands are tackled from different but equally complex positions, with texts exploring how one defines a relationship to a country one feels both intimately connected to yet excluded from. Cultural texts are often places where the conflicts around being both 'British' and 'other' are most eloquently expressed, and where it is possible to challenge received myths about the supposed identity crises from which children and grandchildren of immigrants are said to suffer. To be a member of an 'immigrant' community in Britain is to hold together many identity positions at once: for example, one may call oneself 'black' at a political rally, Gujarati at a social function, and British at the passport control at Heathrow airport, and not necessarily be tormented by competing internal subjective voices. Those of us who grew up puzzled by the wisdom that we were 'torn between two cultures', or that we were the aggressive 'bad' progeny of passive and 'good' parents, share a sense of the enormity of the task of speaking our cultural identities in all their complexities. Although different communities have been pathologised in different ways, and often at the expense of each other, there is still much that is illuminating in reading this literature together. I would suggest that novels as divergent as Hanif Kureishi's *The Buddha of Suburbia*, Atima Srivastava's *Transmission* or Joan Riley's *Romance* can be read in relation to some of these recurring concerns for 'second and third generation immigrants'.

However, while it is possible to read such literature together, the question remains why we would want to do this, as does the question of why we would want to use the *Windrush* celebrations, in part, to reassert the similarity of 'immigrant' experience. After all, the problems of creating a stable 'black' political identity, in its peculiarly British sense of referring to a radical politics of Afro-Asian unity, have been legion, and so perhaps my suggestion could be seen as naive. But it is important to remember that, even if we are not happy with the terminology and the ways in which 'black' has been mobilised in certain political discourses, we should not underestimate the power of collective narratives which speak to people outside of the supposedly secure borders of their 'minority' group.

As we reach the end of the millennium, different 'black' cultures in Britain are coming of age in many ways. New political imaginings, cultural styles and languages open up the spaces where Britishness intersects with varied diasporic heritages, to create vibrant and resilient identities. But at the same time as the repackaging of Britain as 'Cool Britannia' is dependent on a 'black' presence to convey diversity, dynamism and youthfulness, we are under continued threat. Racial attacks are reported to be on the increase and there seems to be a surreptitious return of imagery and iconography which is reappropriating Britishness as 'whiteness'. As total economic and political European union looms closer, we are not able to cross borders with the ease of our white counterparts holding the same passport, and we are subjected to increased surveillance within 'Fortress Europe'. These difficulties are too often met by political strategies from within 'black' communities which appeal to monolithic, reactionary and exclusive definitions of political and cultural communities, such as those coming from varied forms of religious fundamentalism. In the face of all this it seems apposite that the *Windrush* anniversary should remind those 'immigrants' and their descendants of the importance of continuing to find shared spaces and languages of resistance.

F inally, while I have posed the question of being 'in the same boat', the extent to which the metaphor is applicable is questionable. The important point is that we occupy multiple identity positions, and are members of a range of different communities at the same time - a flexibility the metaphor denies. Perhaps another metaphor of migration could capture this flexibility, and more aptly capture the condition we share.

Bibliography

Emecheta, Buchi, *Second-Class Citizen*, Allison and Busby 1974.

Gilroy, Beryl, *Black Teacher*, Cassell 1976.

Kureishi, Hanif, *The Buddha of Suburbia*, Faber and Faber 1990.

Lamming, George, *The Pleasures of Exile*, Allison and Busby 1984 (first published by Michael Joseph, 1960).

Riley, Joan, *Romance*, The Women's Press 1988.

Selvon, Samuel, *The Lonely Londoners*, Longman 1985, first published by Alan Wingate, 1956.

Shan, Sharan-Jeet, *In My Own Name - an Autobiography*, The Women's Press 1985.

Srivastava, Atima, *Transmission*, Penguin 1992.

Syal, Meera, *Anita and Me*, Flamingo 1996.

Christmas cake and calypso

Val Wilmer

Val Wilmer *remembers the music of the* Windrush *generation, and the effect they had on British cultural life.*

I must have been about ten and my brother was just seven when we added a new 'I spy' game to our repertoire. Sitting in the front seat upstairs on the 59 bus, we'd crane our necks in search of black faces and score points for spotting what was still a very rare quarry. It was the early 1950s and an exciting departure from logging car number plates or BSA motorbikes, although even back then, I was instinctively aware that what we were doing was not quite 'on'. As bus top rituals went, this one was a trifle subdued. We had only an inkling of parental disapproval but that was enough, our mother being embarrassed not on her account alone but on behalf of the 'strangers' we counted on these voyages through darkest Brixton.

So shameful is the memory of this childhood game that I had forgotten it until I started writing this essay. I only mention it in order to illustrate the all-encompassing whiteness of the world as I knew it back then. I was three-and-a half years old when the Second World War came to an end and too young to know anything about it. In the part of South London where I grew up, there were no people of colour - at least as far as I knew. We lived in a solid Edwardian 'semi', and I went to a creaking, old-fashioned school run by two women eccentrics. On the day a dog jostled a lunchtime drinker outside the school I learnt my first swear words. When I repeated these at home I was banished to my room for the rest of the evening. Discipline and good manners, chasing butterflies on the bombsites, rhubarb and roast lamb on Sundays, these measured my middle-class life at the end of the 1940s and into the 1950s.

And yet, was it really so white? Even then the contradictions were there. Six years before the *Windrush* chugged up the Thames I'd heard my first black music – in my mother's arms. At least I can remember her singing an old 'southern' style lullaby to my baby brother so I'm certain she would have sung the same song to me. Her mother had probably sung it too, at the start of the century, a hangover from the days when 'blackface' minstrels were a commonplace sight in the streets. The words don't bear repeating, and I know, from having asked her about it years later, that Mum had little real idea of their meaning. The important thing is that in those wartime and post-war years there was nothing unusual in her turning to a black music song-form for making this most intimate of connections.

Black music was to change my life dramatically, but in my pre-teen years the power and the passion of Armstrong and Parker were still unknown. And yet, looking back now I realise that for all the 'absolute' whiteness of my world, there *was* a black presence there, albeit not one that was immediately obvious. Underlying the culture that we whites doubtless would, without thinking, have described as 'our own', there was a hidden world of black influence. Unsurprisingly it revolved mainly round music, its specifics being wrapped up in a kind of mishmash of religion and minstrelsy that was never quite what it seemed. As a child I remember no concert party or church social being complete without at least one 'negro spiritual', and by the age of eleven I had joined the Girl Guides where many songs derived from the same source. Around the campfire we'd lustily sing a guiding version of the spiritual 'This little light of mine', followed closely by 'I ain't gonna grieve my lord no more' and 'On Ilkley Moor bah'tat'. The scouting movement was partly responsible for fostering my internationalist outlook, but to be truthful, some aspects of its songbook were unbelievably racist. I even once attended a scout gangshow where they wheeled out a blacked up Mr Interlocutor and the Bones and a banjo. Come to think of it, it's not surprising that the Black and White Minstrel Show took off on television in the 1960s, it had never been away. And in truth, songs that affirmed and comforted the African people in the days of enslavement have never disappeared from mainstream life. Anyone who has been part of certain folk music circles will know them; they surface in the occasional outburst at sports events, in particular in the convention for singing 'Swing low sweet chariot' at rugby matches.

I don't know how old I was when London's West End lights went on again after the war, but I do remember the excitement of evening trips 'into town' in order to see them. Mugs of Horlicks in raffish milk-bars and being allowed to stay up past 9pm were revolutionary experiences; so too was spotting racing tipster Prince Monolulu in Piccadilly Circus, a black man decked out in head-dress of ostrich feathers, waistcoat and breeches, and busking the cinema queues. But like the man with the roses behind his ear who danced for a handful of pennies and the women selling violets outside the London Pavilion, he was part of the general panorama of streetlife. Nobody told me his name at the time, although I remember seeing him on several occasions. There were sightings of other black individuals too: the anonymous 'African' drummers and dancers who appeared at Christmas circuses, and at the end-of-pier shows we went to on holidays. However, I do know that the first black face I could consciously identify belonged to a woman. She was Adelaide Hall, the distinguished American singer, who had recorded the wordless 'Creole Love Call' with Duke Ellington back in the 1920s. We children were not to know that, of course. When I saw her on stage in a show called *Love from Judy*, I was ten years old and she was playing the inevitable maid.

Just a couple of years on from that trip to the theatre I'd bought my first jazz records. Always curious, I began reading up about this new discovery and made rapid strides in my knowledge. I learnt about the music's New Orleans roots, about King Oliver and Louis, Johnny Dodds and Kid Ory, and saved my pocket money to buy 78 rpm records which could be had second-hand for around two shillings apiece. By one of those leaps of faith known only to teenagers, Louis Armstrong's Hot Five and Seven became a kind of spiritual template for my existence at a time when most of my friends were listening to Elvis. Now when I noticed the *Windrush* contingent while passing through Brixton, I began to wonder just who they were. I don't know how conscious it all was, but I do know that I automatically associated them with New Orleans and Jelly Roll, Bessie Smith and the blues, and wanted to know what was their story. How did they fit into the received tale of the music that began in New Orleans and went 'up-the-river' to Chicago? Not surprisingly, given the increasingly hostile climate that was developing around the new settlers, I was discouraged from finding out at first hand. But with black music becoming increasingly a part of my life, I could not be deflected forever.

Did other white English jazzers ask themselves these same questions? Over the years I've met some who did. Certain aficionados even thought that the new black arrivants could help them appreciate the music more fully as well as, in some kind of essentialist way, explaining themselves to themselves. I know such ideas are now regarded as cliché, that the then commonly held belief that to be black meant being 'hipper than hip' is reductive, but as Windrush style itself becomes a cliché at the end the century, I want to stand back and examine the way in which the burgeoning black presence changed one English life.

Caribbean style became, for some white people, almost as important as the music – even if we wouldn't always admit to this belief in more enlightened times. Larger than life West Indians seemed to me then, leaning on the street corner railings in Brixton, outside the long gone Prince of Wales, twirling their key-chains and spinning a yarn. Hats were very much the order of the day, with padded shoulders and sharp knitwear featuring heavily, and I just knew that these guys were 'cool'. When I started going out to listen to jazz and ran into them as fellow enthusiasts, their personal style - the epitome of relaxation, knowingness and 'hip' - was hard to ignore.

Although I was really quite shy, where the music was concerned I was also precocious. It was hard for a woman to survive on the music scene then, men challenged your presence and would try to break down your resistance in order to deny your integrity. I was fortunate to be befriended by a number of people who wrote about music as well as by several musicians. Through these contacts I found my feet in a difficult world and was enabled to establish an identity as a serious advocate of the music at a time when most women in my position would have fallen by the wayside - that is, gone off and got married. Most importantly, it was through the more perceptive individuals I met, both black and white, that I was encouraged to always think of jazz as being a black creation.

It is not generally realised outside the jazz world, but in the years before and after the war the music's followers often divided into two camps – those who favoured 'black' jazz and those who championed white players. Despite the near universal perception of jazz as something that black people do, for all the lip service paid to equality and the acknowledged innovators, the white British jazz world could, and can still, be shamefully antipathetic to the wider black presence. Where the white proselytisers I met were concerned, there was some racial stereotyping involved in their otherwise positive attitudes – a further legacy from the days of the spirituals and minstrelsy – nevertheless it was because I embraced a belief in vernacular authenticity that I got to know the music's movers and shakers.

There has always been great irony in the racist element that persists in the jazz world, of course, for the Windrush generation was responsible for

'Songs that affirmed and comforted the African people in the days of enslavement have never disappeared from the mainstream'

changing the way in which the British appreciated and responded to black music. Even if differences of aesthetic persisted, the arrivants were a dominant factor in developing the climate of receptivity for African musical expression in all its diversity. For many of us growing up post-war in British cities, our listening was significantly conditioned by the sounds to which the newcomers danced. Revolutionary black music had a similar effect on our parents' generation. They'd responded enthusiastically to jazz and swing. The difference now was that these sounds meant something special for a group of people living here in our midst. From calypso and bebop to ska and rock-steady, black Britons began to make some of the runnings. And while white Merseysiders may have been the conduit whereby much rhythm-and-blues entered the mainstream, it's acknowledged now that black Liverpool seamen were the people who brought those records back from America. Whenever West Indians and Africans danced to this new music, the uptown modern blues, they were doing so not only because those sounds were hip, but because they represented black creativity and positive expression. And, albeit as an outsider, I was fortunate to be part of that movement.

My own Caribbean connections began one afternoon in 1960. I had skived off from college to go to the Wood Green Empire, taking my camera with me. Nat 'King' Cole was rehearsing a TV show, and I was hoping I might get some pictures. I ran into a group of Jamaicans who had just started a magazine and wanted the singer's stamp of approval. They were looking for writers too, and saw me as a likely contributor. The magazine was called *Tropic*, its publisher was Charlie Ross, a one-time bassist and drummer who'd made a few records. The editor was a lifelong jazz enthusiast named Edward Scobie from Dominica; both had been in Britain with the RAF during the war. Scobie would eventually settle in the United States and write *Black Britannica*, a history based on his *Tropic* articles and BBC broadcasts about the black British presence.

Scobie wanted me to do a piece on Joe Harriott, the Jamaican alto saxophonist noted for his fiery and passionate playing. Harriott was an important member of the *Windrush* generation. He arrived in England in 1951 to play at The Festival of Britain and quickly established himself in London jazz circles. During a lengthy illness, he developed a concept of improvisation that freed its participants from some of the strictures of bebop. Each weekend he played at the Marquee, then a jazz club in Oxford Street, so I went there to meet him. I found him involved in a dispute with the club's manager with the result that, instead of interviewing the leader, I ended up hanging out with the band. From that point everything snowballed. His drummer asked me to take publicity photographs of his trio at a little black club where he was playing; his trumpeter befriended me and invited me home. Through these new friendships I got to know about other local black instrumentalists who made a living from music.

The Harriott group were hot and controversial so they attracted a perceptive, and bohemian, audience. At one of their gigs I met a Nigerian sculptor called Lucky and we began to go out together. At home he'd kick off his shoes and dance to what we then called 'modern jazz' records. He loved people such as Kenny Clark and Thelonius Monk, the American *inventors* of bepop, and taught me to recognise their music as a vehicle for personal self-expression as much as the purely serious business of listening. As I ate Lucky's *fufu* and pepper soup, I imbibed a sense of the way that the music meant something quite different for him than it meant to outsiders like me. I was yet to put all this into words, although I do know that as a result of this understanding I began to operate instinctively with this in mind while carving out a career for myself as a writer and photographer. I'd go through many changes in my personal life, yet I always retained a belief in the purity of the music and a feeling for what those early friends and acquaintances showed me. American musicians taught me plenty as well, but the sheer visceral understanding of what it meant to black people to acknowledge the music as being *one's own*, with a value – and values – quite separate from mainstream perceptions, began for me in places like Lucky's Camden Town bed-sit.

When I left college prematurely, Ed Scobie offered me a full-time job on his magazine. I thought it would be the making of me as a journalist but the sobering truth was that they just wanted someone to answer the phone. Nevertheless, installed in their battered shop-front premises in Bell Street off Edgware Road, I made connections with *Windrush* graduates that last to this day. In the winter of 1960-61, with a single paraffin heater for company and the wind whistling round the street-corner, I warmed to a new way of seeing between trips to the little café next door for rice-and-peas and coffee thick with Carnation milk.

A Jamaican trombonist named Herman Wilson helped form my vision. He'd come to Britain in the same band as Joe Harriott and when I met him in Bell Street I invited him home. He arrived wearing his duffel coat and carrying a small pepper plant as a gift for my mother. We'd never seen one before – it was only recently that peppers and aubergines had appeared in the shops after all, no-one knew what they were – and he told us he'd never been in an English home for tea. In Herman's room off the Harrow Road I had another salutary and life-altering experience. His mother had just sent him a cake for Christmas, packed with fruit and dripping with rum. He offered a slice but to my dismay cut the tiniest sliver. Coming from a home where cake always came in fat slices, I thought his action a little on the ungenerous side. It would be ages before I'd realise the ungraciousness of harbouring such thoughts, but I was nineteen years old and had so much to learn. Herman had no need to share something so special, something that was such a lifeline to home. It was his way of recognising my own acknowledgement of him by inviting him home. Only recently, when I was writing a story about the musicians who came on the *Windrush*, we spoke at length. We exchanged memories of those first meetings although I couldn't bring myself to tell him how I felt about the cake. But I've never forgotten my ingratitude. The memory of the rudeness I harboured rises to haunt me now along with visions of playing that numbers game on the buses.

Where the music was concerned, there was a sense in which the *Windrush* generation liberated what was already there. Calypso, after all, was not unknown before the newcomers unpacked their suitcases, any more than were jazz, swing, the gospel songs and the blues. Right back to the Fisk Jubilee Singers who made Queen Victoria cry and the ragtime songs of the turn of the century, black music had always had a strong effect on white lives. Until the *Windrush*, however, it could be dismissed as phenomenon or entertainment. The vivid, the living, Caribbean presence gave it a credence it hadn't previously possessed. Respect for black music did not occur overnight, neither was any kind of sophisticated musical analysis swift to emerge, but the process of understanding began when the calypsonian Lord Kitchener and his fellow passengers put down their roots in this county. They needed the music to ease the process of settlement, and the songs they brought with them provided spiritual sustenance and cultural affirmation.

Initially, Caribbean music captivated and intrigued that section of the jazz audience concerned with authenticity. In time, it became an essential part of the backdrop to the rock-and-roll generation. Even into the 1960s, as white people began embracing the gospel-inspired soul music that grew out of the civil rights struggle, few really 'hip' British homes were without the odd single by the risqué Kitch or his misogynist musical scion, Prince Buster. As both a feminist and a lifelong jazzer, I have to own up at this point and admit that I too was one of those who danced and chuckled along to both 'Dr Kitch' and 'Wreck A Pum-Pum' in that halcyon period. Soon the pioneering *Windrush* 'versions' would be replaced by the reggae nationalism of Bob Marley and Burning Spear, but the contribution of the people who walked down the gangplank at Tilbury half a century ago endures in the lives of those of us who took up their challenge. They inspired us to discover a new way of hearing, of listening and looking. Through this, British people fashioned a new way of being.

The Windrush issue

Postscript

Stuart Hall

The '*Windrush*' file collected here by Gail Lewis and Lola Young, with its varied styles, voices and *genres*, seems to me to do at least three things which distinguish it from much of the otherwise extremely interesting writing which accompanied the celebrations this year to mark the anniversary of the arrival of the *Empire Windrush* at Tilbury in 1948, with its human cargo of Britain's first post-war Caribbean migrants. First, they try to give a sense of the 'irresistible rise of multi-racial Britain' - as Trevor and Mike Phillips put it in their excellent companion volume to the BBC2 series - which the *Windrush* has come to signify from the inside. Several pieces bring vividly back to us what it has actually meant *both* to a generation of Afro-Caribbean people, *and* to the British, Asian and African communities who were, in different ways, central actors in the drama which has unfolded but who, in the event, tended to be somewhat decentred. Secondly, they connect the event irrevocably to the present, to our current situation: writing it as a 'history of the present' not a nostalgic revisiting of the past. Thirdly, they use it as a benchmark against which to make a provisional assessment of how far we have travelled since 1948 along that road which, as the BBC series forcefully reminded us, took a serious dip downwards before it began its slow upward curve.

What they offer on this count seems to add up to neither a simple celebration of change (and a source of complacent British self-congratulation), which the *Windrush* event tended to become, nor a simple confirmation that racism is forever and nothing ever changes - which is a tempting scenario. The collection has, instead, been an occasion to engage in the much more difficult and troubling task of offering an account which steers clear of self-confirming simplifications on either side, and sticks firmly with the complexities, the difficulties, of returning any simple answer to this historic *Windrush* question.

Jackie Kay's short story, recreating the migration experience through the eyes of her heroine, Rose McGuire, Femi Franklin's commentary to his personal photographic archive from the 1940s and 1950s, bringing the Nigeria-London connection into the frame, Roshi Naidoo's piece, reminding us that the *Windrush* 'belongs' to diverse migrant audiences, African and Asian as well as Caribbean, and Val Wilmer's poignant essay on her involvement in the early Black British jazz scene, all brought the *Windrush* experience vividly back to us as a lived experience.

Actually, there are some hidden connections here. Personal photo-albums like Femi's, and the more professional photographs of both the music scene and the early West Indian community by Val Wilmer, alongside the more 'public', heart-stopping images from *Picture Post* and the Imperial War Museum which were on exhibition at the Pitshanger Gallery in Ealing during the *Windrush* season, constitute (as I've remarked elsewhere, in my 'Reconstruction Work', photo-essay) some of the few and most precious remaining parts of the *visual* archive of those early post-*Windrush* days. These had a special poignancy for those of us who migrated to Britain in the early 1950s. The scenes and haunts Val Wilmer recalls were among the very few public (semi-public?) spaces where one did and could go, in the London of the 1950s, to hear the sound and feel the pulse of an authentic Caribbean atmosphere - Joe Harriot and Shake Keane playing, not 'reggae' (which hadn't yet been invented) but modern jazz, at the Marquee in Oxford Street (the luridly fluorescent, half-lit basement where, as it happens the Universities And Left Review Club first held their meetings in the early 1960s) is amongst my earliest musical memories of London.

What moved me especially about Val Wilmer's piece was the sensitivity and courage with which she records how one white English woman, whose voice today remains in some indefinable way distinctly 'English', was deeply re-shaped, not superficially but profoundly and irrevocably, by her encounter with 'the *Windrush* generation': and the hope her story signifies to us all of the possibility of witnessing, even at this late stage in our lifetimes, the astonishing sight of the birth of an authentically post-colonial 'Englishness'.

'The living Caribbean presence', she writes, gave that other world 'a credence it hadn't previously possessed'. Val, who came to know and inhabit this black world better than most black people, will not be surprised to know - but others may be - that it was equally transformatory for young black Caribbean people who had themselves migrated! I had met very few West Indian people other than Jamaicans before I came to London in 1951, when the black migrant presence was still extremely small. I was in open revolt against the middle-class 'colonial' culture and attitudes of my family, from whom, above all, I had 'emigrated'. Still, nothing could assuage that deep ache in the heart for the place one left behind which assails every migrant in the least expected moment. Meeting ordinary folks from the Caribbean in London was, for me, in experience exactly the same as it was for Val Wilmer, but from the opposite spectrum. It was to find 'a presence', as if the 'real' Caribbean I had never found there had come to meet me here.

This *is* the paradigm diasporic experience. The plain fact is that I became 'black' in London, not in Kingston. Roshi Naidoo, in her essay, about the *Windrush's* diverse audiences, not only refers to another key document of this diasporic transition-zone - Sam Selvon's *Lonely Londoners*, which spoke for us all - but quotes a line from George Lamming's *Pleasures Of Exile* which says it all: 'no islander from the West Indies sees himself as a West Indian until he encounters another islander in foreign territory .... In this sense, most West Indians of my generation wore born in England'.

David Sibley on the racialisation of spaces and 'things', and Philip Cole's thought-provoking essay on citizenship and difference, put the *Windrush* experience in broader contemporary context. Sibley's essay reminds us how powerfully urban space has been racialised in the imaginary geographies of race, and how much these fixings of spatial identity are silently carried, like a virus in the bloodstream, in the coded conversations about race which are part and parcel of our everyday discourse. Cole, on the other hand, by setting migration in the context of globalisation, raises profound questions for political theory about the explicit universalism and the covert particularism which have accompanied the liberal, post-Enlightenment, 'Western' discourse on citizenship. He brought to the surface the way the internal bonding of political communities, which is recognised in the struggle to extend citizenship rights to 'everyone', tacitly, assuming that questions of cultural difference have already been resolved, rests upon what is excluded - those who are refused access, who are beyond the frontier - citizenship's constitutive outside. This remind us not only of Paul Gilroy's deconstructions of the hidden interlocking of 'nation' and 'race', but also of the far-too-casual way in which Benedict Anderson - whose notion of nations as 'imagined communities' has been so productive - dismissed the idea that the archaic notion of 'race' and the modern notion of 'nation' could cohabit in the same discursive space.

The other pieces in their different ways plunge us into the complicated and ambiguous waters of the present. Julia Sudbury's essay is one of the most thoughtful attempts to steer a path through the treacherous waters of the intersections between race, gender and sexuality, in the form of the debate between black feminism and (often male-led) black anti-racism, or as she puts it, between gender activism and black masculinity, She wryly notes the way black women, seeking greater independence, have been made 'responsible' for emasculating black men, and how this has been used to police black feminism into line, black feminist struggles becoming the object of reactionary revisionism. There is much to be learned from the way she courageously refuses to be driven to either of the opposing poles of this false binary, and from the care with which she identifies the points at which progressive coalitions can be built across the gender divide, whilst not making concessions either to the collusive silence of the black community ('don't wash your dirty linen in public') or to forms of black homophobia.

> 'Nothing could assuage that deep ache in the heart for the place one left behind'

How far, then, have we come along the road to a multi-cultural society which the arrival of the *Windrush* put so irrevocably on the agenda? Bilkis Malck on English football and the World Cup poses the significant question - not whether, but how much, difference has the 'coming of the margins into representation' made? I liked the way this piece marked *both* the shift towards inclusivity *and* the stubborn persistence of racism – the way the terraces can simultaneously embrace Ruud Gullit and Ian Wright *and* scream racist abuse in a single, ambiguous movement. She seems right to stick with the notion of the continuing deep ambivalence of the British towards an expanded definition of the nation, at least as these movements are reflected in the overwhelming mirror of football. Anne Phoenix's persuasive analysis of how indelibly the present situation is doubly inscribed by the simultaneous vibrancy of hybridisation and the pervasiveness of racism is compelling and important. Everyone will recall that in the very moment when *Windrush* celebration were in full swing, the Official Inquiry into the death of Stephen Lawrence was being convened at the Elephant and Castle. The fact is that neither the one nor the other represent the 'true face' of multicultural Britain. The 'truth' lies with recognising the power and presence of *both* contradictory impulses, together, at the same time – and, Ann Phoenix adds, on the basis of the psychological evidence from her youth interviews, in the same classroom, and sometimes *in the same person*. Far from being mutually exclusive, locked in some permanent binary, Black and White are moveable feasts, which, in a society deeply in transition, not only consistently appear in the same space, but – as she says – are 'readily reconcilable as contradictory subjectivities'.

Just in case anyone is still left with the illusion after reading these essays that the 'irresistible rise of multi-racial Britain' is a simple affair, they should try reading again Gail Lewis's interview with the eloquent twelve-year old, Simon. We speak, glibly, of identity as 'becoming', as a negotiation between past and future; as a way of situating oneself in relation to a complicated 'past' in order to find some point of identification and enunciation in the present. But these abstract terms take life as we watch a mixed-race young 'Black British' boy negotiate his way around the reefs and currents of identity in a post-colonial but still-racist Britain, traiding 'home' against 'home', colour against culture, roots against routes. Here is the young diasporic subject as 'narrator', partly but never completely held by a number of shifting and inter-locking 'stories' and competing loyalties, skilfully warding off the either/ors, holding steadily to the 'both/ands'. It is a remarkable 'performance' of the self, in Judith Butler's phrase, and its grounded knowledge and cosmopolitan openness remains with us as the most eloquently hopeful note in the collection.